P. 40 - We shall be like Him!

BARRIERS
TO
BELIEF

LAYMAN'S THEOLOGICAL LIBRARY
ROBERT MCAFEE BROWN, *General Editor*

Barriers
to
Belief

by
Norman F. Langford

LAYMAN'S
THEOLOGICAL
LIBRARY

THE WESTMINSTER PRESS

PHILADELPHIA

Library of Congress Catalog Card No. 58–6121

Scripture quotations from the Revised Standard Version of the Bible are copyright, 1946 and 1952, by the Division of Christian Education of the National Council of Churches, and are used by permission.

PRINTED IN THE UNITED STATES OF AMERICA

CONTENTS

The religious book market is full of books for "the intelligent layman." Some are an insult to his intelligence. Others are covertly written for professional theologians. A few are genuine helps in communicating the faith.

In this spate of books being thrust at the lay reader, what distinctive place can the Layman's Theological Library claim to hold? For one thing, it will try to remind the layman that he *is* a theologian. The close conjunction of the words "layman" and "theological" in the title of the series is not by chance but by design. For theology is not an irrelevant pastime of seminary professors. It is the occupation of every Christian, the moment he begins to think about, or talk about, or communicate, his Christian faith. The injunction to love God *with all his mind* necessarily involves the layman in theology. He can never avoid theology; if he refuses to think through his faith, he simply settles for inferior theology.

Furthermore, the Layman's Theological Library will attempt to give a *wholeness* in its presentation of the Christian faith. Its twelve volumes cover the main areas of Christian faith and practice. They are written out of similar convictions which the authors share about the uniqueness of the Christian faith. All the authors are convinced that Christian faith can be made relevant, that it can be made understandable without becoming innocuous, and that (particularly in view of the current "return to religion") it is crucially important for the layman to commit himself to more than "religion in general." The Layman's

7

Theological Library, then, will attempt a fresh exploration of
the Christian faith, and what it can mean in the life of twen-
tieth-century man.

But fresh explorations are not always reassuring. There is no
guarantee that " a fresh exploration of the Christian faith " will
clarify. It may confuse. For our exploration may lead us to barriers unknown to us when we were safe in the land of unbelief.

This happens to all of us when we undertake a serious ex-
amination of the claims of Christian faith. We come to believe
in a God whose ways are not our ways — and run headlong
into disturbing questions about the miracles. Or we come to
see that the God of Christian faith is a sovereign Lord who
rules over all — and this creates disturbing perplexities about
predestination. Or we work our way through to a coherent
understanding of our faith — and run up against the greatest
barrier to belief of all, in the form of serious doubts about
whether it really matters what we believe after all.

There are many such barriers. Mr. Langford has selected a
good half dozen of them for extended treatment. In the last
analysis it is not crucially important whether the barriers to the
reader's belief are precisely the same half dozen that are discussed here or not. What is important is that in the following
pages the reader can share with the author in the exciting task
that is laid upon every Christian, the task of being a theologian
himself, working through for himself, with the help of Scripture and the wisdom of the church, a clarification and resolution of some of the problems that impede the clearness of his
vision, the sureness of his faith, and the depth of his commitment. The reader becomes a partner in this task, with the result
that when he has engaged in a prolonged assault on some of the
barriers, he will know how to proceed to deal with further
barriers.

ROBERT MCAFEE BROWN

1

Barriers to Belief: Their Cause and Cure

Every thinking person is likely at one point or another to run into stumbling blocks as he tries to understand Christian doctrine.

It is unfair to make this experience a kind of test of faith, with the implication that if one only " had faith " he would not be perplexed by miracles, or the divinity of Christ, or predestination. On the contrary, it frequently happens that deeply committed Christians have been just as deeply troubled by their inability to comprehend some of the more inscrutable aspects of their faith. A man who has not in any way been seized by the power of faith may not even care what Christian doctrine teaches.

The Need for Clear Thinking

These intellectual difficulties are nevertheless not to be dismissed as though they were of no consequence. For so long as one is unable to think coherently or speak intelligibly about such matters, a shadow that ought not to be there falls across one's wholehearted belief in Jesus Christ. The mind is plagued, either consciously or subconsciously, by haunting doubts as to whether Christian teaching really makes sense. To the outsider, who neither professes Christian faith nor can quite dismiss it wholesale, such problems may lead to the conclusion that Christianity is a mixture of profound insight, tradition- alism, superstition, and downright error.

The existence of intellectual problems is often attributed to the professional theologians, who, as the argument goes, insist on manufacturing complex doctrines in place of "the simplicity of Christ." No doubt there is much theology that is far too sophisticated, but this diagnosis of the trouble is inadequate just the same. There would be no need for theologians if every- thing in the Bible were self-evident. The church has had to be busy about theology, from the earliest times until now, precisely because the Bible itself — and Jesus most of all — creates dif- ficulties that the theologian must try to solve. God's ways to men, as presented in the Scriptures, are clothed in a mystery that confuses the human intellect. Granting that God's ways are past finding out, and his secret counsels hidden in his own in- finite depths, it is nevertheless the duty of Christian teachers to describe the substance of their faith as clearly and systemati- cally as they can. In other words, theologians are trying, not to make things more difficult than they already are, but rather to show how the raw material of what is in the Bible can best be understood.

Although many classical statements of Christian theology exist, we cannot allow ourselves to rest in these as though the last word had been spoken. Obviously, if such statements were sufficient, everyone would be intellectually satisfied and all problems would thereby be solved. In every age it is necessary to get a fresh grasp of what Scripture teaches, and not merely repeat what has been said — however competently and suitably — in former times. By the same token, in every age it is neces- sary to attack these problems in such a way that the valid in- sights of traditional theology are not lost or denied.

Although the above comments apply to the whole field of

theology, it is clear that some problems are more acute than others and therefore demand more intensive treatment. In the chapters following, a selection has been made of some of the most difficult doctrines that theology has to tackle. Many more could be added. But to a large number of people the matters dealt with in this book are among the most baffling to be found in Scripture and theology.

Nothing at the heart of Christian faith can be solved in intellectual terms alone. In the last resort faith has to accept the presuppositions on which we shall be working in this book. The chief of these is one that has always characterized mature Protestantism: that the Bible is to be taken seriously as declaring the Word of God, and that whatever we think or say must be tested in the light of what the Scriptures teach. Even if this presupposition is not accepted, however, it does not follow that what can be said about what is discussed in the following chapters (always taking the Bible with full seriousness) need be irrational. For there is more *sense* to Christian doctrine than often seems to meet the eye. In the case of every one of the questions dealt with here, the doctrine hangs together and ought — if rightly presented and understood — to command intellectual respect if nothing else.

All Thinking Has a Pattern

Although a glance at the Table of Contents reveals a rather miscellaneous selection of subjects, this does not mean that the book is just a collection of essays on assorted themes. No one can think about theological matters, or anything else, without having some system of thought in the back of his mind. The reader will soon find that in these chapters there are recurring expressions, persistent turns of thought, and a particular approach to Scripture.

The recurring theme which binds these chapters together is that of *God breaking into human life and interrupting it in unexpected ways*. We shall speak again and again, in varying language but with the same fundamental thought in mind, of God acting in unanticipated ways and taking our lives toward an outcome that only God himself could have either imagined or brought to pass.

It need cause no surprise that this is so. For our human thinking is seldom, if ever, really " miscellaneous." That is to say, we think about anything and everything on the basis of certain ideas, traditions, prejudices, personal feelings, and the like. Moreover, how we think about anything and everything is deeply influenced by how we were educated and brought up. Basically, we do not think one way about one subject, and in some totally different fashion about something else. Somewhere, at least underneath our conscious thought, there is consistency. We have some kind of mind-set, some kind of philosophy of life, that governs all our thoughts and even our emotions. If we are intellectually offended at the miracle stories of the Bible, for example, what produces this reaction will probably affect us in regard to the divinity of Jesus, heaven and hell, or any other mental hurdle that confronts us as we read the Scriptures. If it is our " scientific " outlook that raises problems about the miracle accounts, this same outlook will in some manner color our thinking about the rest of theology. Rejecting this one element in Scripture and Christian theology, we may be led on to question the divinity of Jesus, or predestination, or even why belief matters at all. There is always something within ourselves that makes for an underlying consistency of viewpoint.

Likewise, in the chapters to follow, the author inevitably follows the underlying consistency of his own viewpoint. Other ways of approaching these various questions could certainly be devised. Whoever devised them, however, would be following some particular pattern of thought. It is hoped that what is attempted here will cast some light on what Scripture is telling us throughout its various difficult teachings. Indeed, the hope goes farther, and ventures to trust that by showing the fundamental witness that all Scripture bears, the barriers to belief will begin to dissolve.

For it can be assumed that the Bible is not a collection of unrelated peculiarities, and that even when it seems most peculiar it is faithful to itself. The consistency of the Bible, in presenting us over and over again with *the radical and unexpected acts of God,* is what brings order out of apparent chaos. At first glance it would appear that the " chaos " of theology is caused by God's habit of doing that which is most surprising (and so not simply " reasonable "). A second glance, however, is more discerning. It sees that what makes the Bible and theology meaningful and exciting is that God constantly breaks in upon human life in his own way, which is not our way.

There is no neat formula by which we can solve our theological problems. The nearest thing to a " formula " would be simply this: *God is free.* In the following studies we shall see the freedom of God illustrated. Perhaps we shall tremble at it. Let us hope that above all we can rejoice in it.

2

How to Understand the Miracles

Nowadays everything wonderful is called a miracle — everything, it would appear, except those events described as miracles in the Bible. We hear a great deal about the miracle of birth, the miracle of growth, the miracle of spring, the miracle of healing, the miracle of the beauty of the dew upon the grass. At the same time, the miracles that Scripture says that Jesus did have been so downgraded that we hesitate to believe in them at all unless we can " explain " them.

The modern " miracles " referred to above have to do with natural phenomena, and sometimes (for example, in the case of the " miracle drugs " discovered by scientists) with human achievements. This use, or misuse, of the term is very different from what the Bible means by miracles. A miracle in the Bible is an event that is *not* within the normal chain of causes and effects. It is an event that cannot be explained by anything short of the direct intervention of God himself, bringing about some result that could not normally have been expected. This applies even to such an occurrence as the east wind that drove back the sea and let the Israelites escape from Egypt. The writer of the account tells us that God himself had intervened: " The Lord caused the sea to go back by a strong east wind." (Ex. 14:21.) Without his special action, no way of escape from the Egyptians could have been anticipated. This is hardly what we have in mind when we speak of the " miracle of spring."

Perhaps a bad conscience in part accounts for our habit of calling so many things miraculous when we really mean that they are simply wonderful. For one cannot read much of the Bible, especially the New Testament, without coming upon miracle stories. The life and substance goes out of such stories when we insist on being incredulous about anything a scientist cannot see as part of natural law. So we grope around for a stopgap — for something *both* natural *and* wondrous, like birth or growth, that we are not embarrassed to call a " miracle." In that way we too can believe in miracles without violating common sense! On the other hand, to believe in the miracles of the Bible seems to defy all that science has taught us about a reliable universe. It defies, furthermore, any theological notions we may have formed about God working through natural law and not otherwise.

Some Blind Alleys

So acute is the difficulty for many a person that no end of theories have been devised in order to get around the problem of the Biblical miracles. The simplest solution is just to say that no miracle ever occurred at all. However, as this wipes out so much of the Scriptural record (in particular, important sections of the Gospels), not many Christians are prepared to treat the Bible quite so rudely.

Various less radical approaches have been proposed. Some would say that Jesus performed his acts of healing by the power of suggestion; that what happened was due to a change in the sick person's state of mind. This is made more plausible by what doctors have since learned about the way our mental attitude affects state of health. (This theory, of course, is only applicable to miracles of healing, and it is recognized that the

Bible records many other kinds of miracles as well.)

It has also been suggested that ancient people, less observant than we, jumped to conclusions that would have been seen as unwarranted had all the facts been known. For example, some would say that Lazarus was not dead at all, but only in a trance, and that the disciples mistook his condition for actual death. (See John, ch. 11.)

Still another view is that incidents which were not in themselves especially remarkable were magnified as they were told by word of mouth in the years before the Gospels were written. The stories grew, until these events came to be considered supernatural, and by the time the Gospel writers went to work, such occurrences were ready to appear as full-blown miracles.

Another opinion is that Jesus, in his superior wisdom, applied higher laws of nature as yet undiscovered by lesser men. Exponents of this view often go on to predict that in time to come these higher laws will be generally known, so that Jesus' miracles can not only be reproduced but even surpassed. The wonders of modern medicine are sometimes pointed to as evidence that mankind is advancing toward the powers displayed by Jesus.

Why the Alleys Are Blind B 9/23

In evaluating these and similar views, we should keep in mind that such theories are mainly designed to explain Jesus' mighty works, and tend to ignore the miracles of the Old Testament. This implies that only the miracle stories of the Gospels are to be taken seriously at all; and although these miracles are undoubtedly the most numerous and significant, we shall have to inquire later on if the Biblical idea of a miracle, whenever it appears, is not intended to represent something of vast importance for our understanding of the whole of Scripture.

At all events, the fatal weakness in every method of rationalizing the miracles is the underlying assumption that the Biblical writers did not know what they were talking about. Now although it was no doubt easier to accept miracles before scientific ways of thinking had gained so firm a hold on the human mind, ancient writers did not need to be instructed in modern science to discern that many of the events they recorded were contrary to natural law. Put more bluntly, the reason the Biblical writers emphasize the miracles is precisely that these things did not, in their opinion, come to pass through purely natural causes. If anything is obvious, it is that the Scriptural writers believed that very extraordinary things had occurred. The authors of the four Gospels would certainly have quickly lost their interest in Jesus' acts of healing if they had supposed for a moment that what such acts highlighted was merely the power of Jesus' personality. If several different kinds of explanation can be offered for several different kinds of miracles, all of them quite easy to comprehend, there was little object in making much of the miracles at all.

It is perfectly apparent that these writers thought they could not get the gospel message across without stressing the miraculous. Even if we choose to think that these ancient authors were mistaken, it is at least reasonable to ask why miracles loom so large in the Biblical story. What did the writers think the miracles meant? What were they trying to say to us through emphasizing the miracles? Before we explain the miracles away on the ground that people of Biblical times were simply ignorant of natural laws, and a bit superstitious in the bargain, it would be wise to look more closely at the Bible's point of view.

Miracle or Magic?

Before we can hope to get to the bottom of this matter, there is one common source of confusion that must be cleared away.

This is the habit of regarding the miracles as identical with *magic,* and thus out of place in a modern man's view of what is possible in our universe. The truth of the matter is that miracle and magic have nothing in common. For magic, if there were any such thing, would claim to be a kind of occult or mystic science that students of the subject could learn to practice by their own resources. A Biblical miracle, on the other hand, is not controlled, or in any sense done, by any man: it is an unexpected *act of God.*

Until fairly recent times the idea of magic has fascinated the human mind. Even today it can hardly be said that this preoccupation with supernatural matters is a thing of the past. It certainly lives on in fairy tales and ghost stories, and most of us take a childlike delight in the uncanny. During World War II there was an immense spread of superstitious cults of the very kind that the Bible would most roundly condemn. Teacup readers and crystal-gazers did a land-office business among people who naturally wondered what the future held for them. In England, with many families mourning their dead, spiritualism enjoyed a new burst of popularity in the war years. Astrologers have never lacked a following for their peculiar " science."

All this would get short shrift from the standpoint of the Bible. To bring back the spirits of the dead was, by Biblical standards, a forbidden art — witness the witch of Endor! (The story is found in I Sam., ch. 28.) Whatever the Bible means by miracles, it is certainly not suggesting a practice of black arts known only to the initiated. A significant story is to be found in Luke 11:14-23. We are told that Jesus was casting out a demon from a man who was dumb. Seeing Jesus cast out devils, his enemies whispered it about that he was in league with the devil — in effect, practicing some species of black magic. To his foes, it appeared that Jesus was guilty of witch-

craft. Jesus heatedly replied that he was working, not with, but
against the devil. So far from trying to disturb men by bringing anything sinister into their lives, he was bringing the power
of the good God into the world to set things right. "But if it
is by the finger of God that I cast out demons, then the kingdom of God has come upon you" (Luke 11:20). Jesus is "a
strong man" (see vs. 21-22), overcoming the power of evil in
every form that it takes.

This power, the power of Christ, is not an occult art. It is
the very power of God breaking into human life. Christ's
works represented the strength of the Creator God, who made
the creation good to begin with and in Jesus was at work to
make it good again. In Jesus, no one less than God himself had
taken a strong hand in human affairs.

Here we are in a different world of thought from that of
magic. Magic is a human fantasy — dangerous, if not absurd.
Miracle is God himself acting, God at work to redeem human
life. Thus the point about a miracle is not that it is an example
of tampering with supernatural forces, which may or may not
exist. The point about a miracle is that it is what God does. It
is a *free* act of God, who is *free* to act according to his own
will. It is an act of the same God who, in the beginning, said,
"Let there be light," and light appeared; and who, in Jesus,
said to the blind, with equal effectiveness, "See!" and they
saw again.

This "Interrupted" Life

It was suggested at the beginning of this chapter that the
miracles are a stumbling block to modern men because we have
learned to think of life as a chain of causes and effects. In other
words, we know that every ordinary event must have some
rational cause. Conversely, every cause may be expected to

have some understandable effect. All this is true of life as we know it.

But the very point of the miracles is that they *interrupt* life as we know it, and give it either a new turn or a promise of some outcome different from what we would anticipate. That is the Bible's viewpoint as to miracles, and that is why the Bible makes so much of them. Something breaks in, at least momentarily, to transform the world. The so-called " explanations " of the miracles sketched above when we were exploring blind alleys try to make the miracles plausible by accounting for them in ways that do not disturb the ordinary relationship of cause and effect. The Bible, on the contrary, is interested in the miracles, not as wonders or as occult acts, but as instances of God moving in upon us creatively.

Much is made, in modern habits of thought, of the reliability of the universe. Sometimes we comfort ourselves, in the midst of trial and tribulation, by recollecting that God moves, not in a mysterious way, but through natural laws that he laid down and that can be forever trusted. It is a little difficult to understand the virtue of this alleged reliability. If the sick regularly die, if the blind regularly lack eyesight, if sinful men regularly remain in sin, this is a regularity with which we could surely dispense. Life, sight, righteousness — these are things that we surely would desire even at the expense of dependable natural laws.

How much we would prefer such gifts — no matter how unexpected they might be — is demonstrated in our prayers. Few of us, when confronted with real danger or trouble, are prepared to rest content with the inevitable operation of natural law. In our distress we cry out to God for deliverance, not supposing that in each and every case he will bring us through unscathed, but certainly hoping that *this* will be the time when our very concrete prayers will be answered favorably in ways beyond our understanding. Every such prayer is in effect a confession that we *do* believe in miracles, or at least that we want a miracle on our behalf.

This is no sign of weakness. For the whole story of the Bible is the story of God breaking into human life with surprising and beneficial results. We do well to seize hold of the miracles of forgiveness and resurrection — the greatest hopes held forth by Scripture — not just in a general way but every day and in every concrete fashion that we can imagine. It will be recalled that at the grave of Lazarus the dead man's sister said (rather mechanically and very joylessly) that Lazarus would no doubt rise at the last day. The raising of Lazarus demonstrated, among many other things, that God is a God of action. The normal course of life and death was spectacularly interrupted, and Lazarus, at the sound of the sovereign word of God, was alive again. Even the dead need not stay dead if Jesus Christ willed otherwise.

The entire life of Jesus was an " interruption " of the way human history was going. Significantly, his career on earth begins and ends with a miracle. It begins with the miracle of the virgin birth. Many have wondered why Matthew made so much of it, and why some theologians have been so insistent on this point. The miracle of the virgin birth, as presented in Scripture, and as emphasized by theology, is not intended merely to " prove " that there was something extraordinary about the circumstances of Jesus' birth. It is not intended to mystify the believer, much less to serve as a kind of test of faith. The virgin birth is to be understood as signifying something new, something different, some different course for human nature, now being introduced on earth. Here is a *break* with the unhappy chain of past human events.

Jesus' career ends with the miracle of the resurrection, in which our death-bound existence is given a new hope and a

different direction. Here we see the real potentialities of God
becoming man. Something very eventful, something revolutionary, was instituted by the very fact that there was such a
person as Jesus Christ — God in human flesh. Incarnation, resurrection — these are the basic terms that illuminate all else
that we are told about Jesus Christ. In the light of the incarnation, which is the greatest miracle of all, and in the light of the
resurrection, without which the New Testament would not
hang together, we see how suitable it is that along the path
of his earthly life Jesus should mark his career with many acts
of God's power. These acts declared the redemption that was
being brought to pass by him who was born of a virgin and
rose from the dead. This is the great interruption which reverses the course of our life in the most ultimate way possible — reverses it from sin toward goodness, from death to
life eternal.

Acts of Love

Such is the essential clue that theology can offer for understanding what the Bible intends to tell us through its miracle
accounts. We can see the same clue in a different fashion when
we consider that the miracles of the Gospels are *acts of love*.
Jesus heals; he gives sight to the blind and hearing to the deaf;
he restores men who are lost in life, and he raises the dead. It
is important to note that when John the Baptist, plagued with
doubts as to whether Jesus was really the Messiah, sent his
own disciples to investigate, Jesus not only pointed to these
acts of power and compassion but in the same breath com-
mented that the poor had the gospel preached to them. (Matt.
11:2-6.)

This last phrase underlines the compassionate character of
Jesus' whole ministry, including his deeds. Steadfastly he re-

fused to " prove " he was the Messiah by performing works to excite wonders. No proof was possible by astonishing people by a display of power. No proof is possible today by stressing the miracles. Unless the miracles recounted in the New Testament are understood as witnessing to God's *love* in Christ, it will avail nothing to emphasize the supernatural *power* shown in these events. For when the accent is on power alone, the reaction will be one of two kinds: Either people will refuse to believe that any miracles took place, on the ground that God does not work that way; or else they will fall into the trap of seeing Jesus as a wonder-worker, which is the very thing that he abhorred.

It is of course foolish to speak of believing in Christ apart from the miracles, for we know him only through the New Testament, from which the miracle stories are inseparable. Yet in his words to the disciples of John the Baptist, Jesus did not refer to his mighty deeds in terms of power, but rather in terms of love. He simply pointed out the good things, the redemptive things, he was doing, and asked to be accepted just as he was — whether or not it was evident that he was the Messiah. He offered no proofs. He simply called for faith in him.

No one can " prove " anything about Jesus' divine-human nature. Only faith knows the love of " God [that] was in Christ, reconciling the world unto himself." But when faith holds to Christ, not as a wonder-worker but as infinite Love incarnate, the miracles take on meaning. What might otherwise appear to be merely occult wonders (or delusions) are seen to be instances of love going forth to change human destiny. The *humanitarian* nature of the Gospel miracles is thus an essential key to understanding why they took place and why they are reported in the Bible at all. These are good deeds done for men in their distress, and therefore testimonies of the gracious concern of God for his creatures. They are testimonies to the fact that love is power.

All this can readily be said about the miracles of Jesus. But when we turn back to the Old Testament, what is the situation? It is certainly not so obvious that every miracle reported there had a loving intention. When by many eventful deeds God at last overawed Pharaoh, and delivered the Jews through the Red Sea, he was merciful to the Jews — but not so kind to the Egyptians. The people of Israel escaped, but the soldiers of Egypt were swallowed up. (See Ex., ch. 14.) When Elijah demonstrated the power of his God and the impotence of Baal, in the contest as to who should bring fire from heaven to destroy the sacrifice, violence followed: this was no gentle miracle. (See I Kings, ch. 18.) So throughout the Old Testament we read of what the psalmist suitably calls the " terrible acts " of God. His intervention in the case of the Old Testament story often brought death and havoc. Are these deeds of love?

To understand these and similar Old Testament miracles, we must remember that they are part of the preparation for the coming of Jesus Christ. We must remember that God's control over history in those ancient times was designed to make it possible for Israel to change the course of this world's affairs. In stern and rugged times God *acted* — sometimes in ways to make men marvel, sometimes simply by his governing power over world history. Moreover, he acted appropriately for every age. What impressed the ruler of Egypt in Moses' time was a demonstration of wonderous might, for the Pharaoh was a man of power himself. These things happened long centuries before Christ.

The witness of Scripture in the Old Testament moves inexorably toward *the* great event which altered everything — the appearance of Jesus Christ. In order that his mighty love might at length be manifest throughout the world, much must precede his coming. These earlier events all point toward what is to come. Jesus Christ gives them their real meaning. He makes permanently real what was hinted at in the Old Testament. The deliverance from Egypt foreshadows the miraculous deliverance of mankind from sin and death. The fire from heaven which vindicated the faith of Israel was such a fire as was set burning on the altar of Calvary where the true Victim offered himself as a sacrifice acceptable to his Father. Only in the light of the New Testament can we rightly read the Old. Only in the light of almighty love can we see where the long and often lurid story of the Old Testament is taking us. *We* do not have to justify the strange events we read about in the Old Testament: Jesus Christ has amply justified them.

Reading the Signs

All that has been said in this chapter brings us inevitably to our final point. It can be stated briefly. The miracles in the Bible are *signs,* and are sometimes so described in the New Testament.

What is a sign? In everyday life it is something that points on to something else. The sign at the crossroads, telling where each fork in the road leads, is there not to decorate the landscape but to show the traveler where he is and where he is going. The sign outside a store is there not for its own sake, but to announce that there are goods to be bought inside.

No human figure of speech is adequate for the great matters of the Bible, but perhaps these rough comparisons may give some conception of what is meant by saying that the miracles are signs. The works that Jesus did, point to who he was and to what he was doing. He did not set out to be a physician who would cure all the sick folk of Palestine. He laid his healing hands on but a few. However, the healings that he did perform, point to the new, redeemed life that he came to usher in — the life where there would be no more sorrow or sinning, no pain and no harm and no death.

Likewise, when he stilled the waves that overwhelmed his disciples with fear, he declared himself Lord of nature. When a multitude was fed with a few loaves and fishes, he showed what an abundance of spiritual food he was able to provide by his own self-sacrifice. Each miracle must be considered in its own right, to determine what it says to us about Jesus Christ. The problem is not " miracles," but discovering the message each miracle in the record bears. It is the same with the mighty acts of God in the Old Testament; each must be interpreted in the light of the whole Biblical story.

The question is not, Could it have happened so? The question is always: Why is this event recorded? What does it mean? To read the signs, to discern the meaning — that is the task of the reader of Scripture. Like all signs, each speaks of something. It speaks of something that belongs to the Bible's word to us. If there is a riddle about the miracles, it does not pertain to whether or not they happened, but to what each one signifies.

To speak of the miracles in general is difficult, because each must be interpreted as it stands. As a summary, however, of most of what has been said in this chapter, perhaps the following will serve:

The miracles mean that almighty love interrupts human life, as a sign of what God has done, is doing, and will complete, to save us from what we are and make us over into what we were created to be.

CHAPTER

3

THE DIVINITY OF JESUS

It is not strange that the Author of our faith, Jesus Christ himself, should also be the author of the greatest intellectual dilemmas that confront the reasoning mind. For from the days of the early church until now Christians have claimed that Jesus was nothing less than God in human flesh. Such a proposition cannot be proved in a scientific way. Reason alone cannot hope to comprehend it .

" In the beginning was the Word, and the Word was with God, and the Word was God. . . . All things were made through him." (John 1:1, 3.) Thus does the writer of the Fourth Gospel begin his testimony to a poor man known as Jesus of Nazareth. The apostle Paul wrote many words about Jesus, so sweeping in their claims that they could rightly be applied only to someone who was truly God. The Nicene Creed, composed little more than three centuries after Jesus lived on earth, declared what the church professes to believe to this very day. It asserted that our Lord Jesus Christ was "begotten of his Father before all worlds, God of God, Light of Light, Very God of Very God . . . of one substance with the Father. . . ."

Christians have always believed these things about Jesus, and yet at the same time they have always been trying to find out what they mean. The faith that Jesus is God incarnate has

27

always been the central claim of Christianity. But we cannot dismiss the matter as though nothing more needed to be said. In what sense, after all, was Jesus really God in human flesh? In a way, the question of " what manner of man is this " is veiled in mystery. Yet we cannot suspend our mental faculties when we come to this all-important question. Precisely because our claims about Jesus are so central to our faith, we are called upon to exert ourselves with special vigor in order to think and speak about him as intelligibly as we can.

The Solution That Solves Nothing

Some have thought that if we only abandoned our claim that Christ is God incarnate, we would have no more problems in understanding him. But this kind of " solution " will not help in the least. Even if Jesus were no more than the greatest of all founders of world religions, the most righteous man ever to walk the earth, the wisest of moral teachers, and all the other things that admiring non-Christians are glad to call him, we would still have a vast number of questions to consider.

" How," we would then have to ask, " did it happen that he gave the impression to his followers that he was immeasurably more than that? Why have theologians from earliest times been forced to devote so much energy and ingenuity to putting into systematic shape what the New Testament tells us or implies about Jesus Christ? If the gospel record were mostly fabrication or illusion, how would we account for its perpetual power in leading people to believe what it says? Were the writers who set down the story of Christ (sometimes in rather rough language) the really creative geniuses in the case, the ones who succeeded in magnifying Jesus into something more than he was? If so, what was the secret of *their* success? And if we take more or less seriously the recorded accounts of Jesus' ministry, how can we reconcile our own portrait of what was simply a rather extraordinary man with what we find in Scripture? Would we not be compelled to set aside, or at any rate to discount and revise, considerable portions of the Gospels in order to validate any conception of a ' purely human ' Jesus? "

Problems for the Thoughtful Christian

Something of this dilemma has already been referred to in our chapter on the miracles. In this present chapter we shall extend our discussion to other aspects of the interpretation of Christ — aspects that have given rise to all kinds of intellectual quandaries for people who feel the need of thinking through what they believe.

To do this takes us into the basic question of what is meant by Christ being both human and divine, which from the start of the Christian era has been at the root of all theological speculation concerning our Lord. Manifestly we cannot in one chapter attempt a full-scale discussion of the nature of Christ. (In another volume of this series, *The Meaning of Christ*, by Robert Johnson, the fundamental matters are presented.) At the same time, we cannot come to grips with the vexing difficulties that plague us without in our own way touching upon some basic issues.

This problem of what is meant by the divinity of Jesus gets embarrassingly concrete in at least three ways. To be specific, a person is apt to reflect along these lines:

" If Jesus was God, he must have been able to know everything. He must also have been able to do anything he wished. But if he was a man, he couldn't have known everything, much less have done everything he would have wanted to do. Was he God or was he man when it came to what he knew and what he could do? " Then there is a second question that is something like the first. It is this:

"God never changes. Men, however, are different: they change and develop as they go through life. They mature, not only in body but also in mind and spirit. As for Jesus, if he was God, presumably he knew where he was going and what he was going to do long before it happened. But as a man, surely he must have gone through a process of development like other men. Did he change, as a man would, or was his course all laid out for him as you would expect with God?"

Still a third question, of a slightly different kind, occurs. It runs like this:

"If Jesus was God, he could not have had any sin. But if he was a man, with our human nature, you would imagine that he would fall into at least a few faults and errors. What kind of man would it be who was sinless? Or on the other hand what kind of God would it be who was tainted with sin? Which was he, then, God or man? And how could he possibly be both?"

Let us look at these problems. Perhaps none of them exactly haunts us in our sleep. Yet questions like these are symptoms of a very basic concern we all feel about what it means to assert that Jesus is in some way both human and divine.

Problem One: Jesus' Knowledge and Power

We had better state again the terms of this first dilemma. If Jesus was God, as Scripture and theology apparently teach, how could he have had any limitations whatsoever — including limitations on his knowledge or power? But if he was a man, how could he be otherwise than limited as to what he knew and what he could do?

Questions like this are not as academic as they may sound on first hearing. For our approach to such a problem reveals the way in which our whole thinking about Jesus is slanted. If we are solely preoccupied with his *divinity*, for example, we will back away from any thought that Jesus lacked the power to do anything he desired or the capacity to know everything there is to know. But if we are solely preoccupied with his *humanity*, we can easily settle for the belief that he was simply a man among men, a child of his time, and without any characteristics that were more than human.

Not a few Christians, and usually ones who pride themselves on being " orthodox," see Jesus as so mysteriously divine that they are scarcely able to admit that he had any human qualities at all. They suppose, for example, that anything known to God the Father was automatically known to Jesus, so that he was by no means confined to what his contemporaries knew in the field, let us say, of science. They shrink from recognizing the real torment of soul that the Gospels say he went through as he faced his great decisions, and are so impressed by what he divinely accomplished through his death that they fail to appreciate the very human agony, the blood and sweat and tears, that went into the suffering of what by all accounts was a rather sordid kind of execution.

These " orthodox" (and certainly sincere and believing) Christians might be surprised to learn that they have, to all intents and purposes, fallen into the trap of one of the earliest heresies of the Christian church. A heresy is an opinion at variance with orthodox views; and an ancient heresy that in one way or another has been repeated through the centuries is technically known as Docetism. The Docetists (so called from a Greek word meaning to " seem " or " appear ") also were offended at the thought of the humanity of Jesus. In ancient times it was inconceivable to most persons that God — even if he should assume human flesh — should be subjected to any sort of limitations. Most repugnant of all was the thought that in any form whatsoever God could suffer and die. Hence the Docetists taught that Jesus was not actually flesh and blood, but only *seemed* to be so. Behind this illusory appearance of being human, a supernatural being was masked.

Thus the sufferings of Jesus were interpreted by these heretics as being only for the sake of outward appearance. God himself was not touched by human emotions, sensations, much less by any limitations. It is difficult to see how a modern insistence on Jesus' divinity, at the expense of any real humanity, is substantially different from this heresy of ancient times. Just as the idea of God incarnate laboring under any kind of handicaps was repulsive to many in early times, so these handicaps are consciously or unconsciously rejected by the Docetists of our own day who boast of their orthodoxy.

Equally if not more widespread is the preoccupation in modern times with the " purely human " Jesus. Many have wanted a picture of Jesus that contains nothing to exceed our understanding. Hence, we have had plenty of so-called biographies of Jesus, which dwell upon his supposed childhood (about which we know little), his growing up, the conditions in which he lived, his emotions and frustrations and hopes and disappointments. It is more difficult to name any ancient heresies that obviously correspond to this attitude than in the case of the opposite viewpoint which was so clearly expressed by Docetism. Suffice it to say that certain heresies did arise which by one means or another tried to take the bite out of the New Testament teaching that " the Word " — that is, Jesus — " was God."

What best serves our present purpose is to note that the whole problem of Jesus' divinity in modern days arises in an interestingly different form from the problem as seen in the early days of the church. Ancient men could not comprehend how God could enter into our common, earthly life. The dignity of God seemed to be compromised by such a notion. The problem then was to imagine *how God could become man*. For that reason people who could not imagine it at all devised various and conflicting views that represented Jesus as either more than human or less than God. Nowadays the problem is somewhat turned around. Our difficulty is to see *how a man could reasonably be regarded as God*. Thus many have been glad to forget about any transcendent qualities that the New Testament attributes to Jesus, and to look upon him as just the same as ourselves though admittedly superior in mentality and character.

Paul Gives the Clue

Before pursuing the first of our problems any farther, much less tackling the others, we need the clearest Scriptural light we can get on all such questions. Fortunately Paul has provided the basic clue in one of the most crucial of New Testament passages. So vital is this passage that the greater part of it must be quoted in full:

"Have this mind among yourselves, which you have in Christ Jesus, who, though he was in the form of God, did not count equality with God a thing to be grasped, but emptied himself, taking the form of a servant, being born in the likeness of men. And being found in human form he humbled himself and became obedient unto death, even death on a cross. Therefore God has highly exalted him and bestowed on him the name which is above every name, that at the name of Jesus every knee should bow. . . ." (Phil. 2:5-10.)

This passage teaches what is technically known as the kenosis of Christ, from a Greek word that means "emptying." After first asserting that Christ was indeed God, Paul goes on to say that Christ was not jealous about his rights but "emptied him-

self " that he might be " born in the likeness of men." In this
human form, Jesus Christ completely subjected himself to
the will of his Father, and died on the cross under the most
abject circumstances: on which account the Father has exalted
his Son to the highest place.

This is a very carefully phrased passage. On the one hand,
the *humanity* of Jesus is asserted without qualification. He indeed emptied himself, becoming a man and in fact a servant.
He came to us in a form that was not recognizable as God.
This self-emptying was not a piece of play-acting, by which
Jesus only seemed (as the Docetists taught) to be human. He
really divested himself of the self-evident marks of divinity.
He carried this so far that he died the death of a common crim-
inal, which, all things considered, was a quite unlikely fate
for a god. What counted, in the mind of Christ, was not to
display himself in the splendors of God, but to serve mankind.
And this necessitated his death.

But Paul does not let it rest there. He avoids depicting Christ
as " just another man." When he speaks of Christ's being
" obedient," he means obedient *to the Father*. The Father's will
is reflected in him and done by him, even to the uttermost.
*Thus God is continually present in him, though to the eyes
of men he is in " the form of a servant."* This self-emptying, or
self-humiliation, turns out in the end to be the way in which
God completely expresses himself; and by virtue of what Jesus
was and did on earth, he is recognized as Lord of all creation.

Real Limitations

This passage from Paul serves to throw a bright light on the
story told in the Gospels. We have before us the account of a
man who can truly be described as " the carpenter of Nazareth," as " the man of Galilee." The qualities and limitations

that are common to all men are underscored in the Gospels. There is no picture of a superman in the Gospel narratives.

In the light of what we have been saying, we need not shrink even from regarding Jesus as in a very real sense a child of his time. If he really emptied himself and became an actual man, no doubt he shared the limited knowledge available to his contemporaries, and held opinions (about science, for example) that were prevalent in his day. He explicitly disavowed knowing when the day of the Lord would take place. (Mark 13:32.) If he really emptied himself and became an actual man, there seems no reason to imagine that he could do whatever he wished, that he could control every human situation. He was compelled to leave all this in the hands of his Father. Indeed, the Gospel accounts stress this also — for they make it exceedingly plain that he could not achieve during his earthly life what he most wished to accomplish, namely, the conversion of Israel to himself. He could not persuade even the disciples of what he was trying to teach them.

Not " Just Another Man "

These limitations were part and parcel of the humanity he bore. No limitations — no true humanity: that is a self-evident proposition. But in this we are not saying that he was " just another man." For the question follows, *Who was this* who " emptied himself "? To be sure, we cannot penetrate into the secrets of what preceded, in eternity, the mortal career of Jesus of Nazareth. But there had been someone there — someone there to empty himself, to become nothing for our sakes, to enlist, as it were, in the ranks of humanity. This was not just another child who happened to be born and happened to grow up and happened to become a landmark in world history. He had his unique character and prerogatives from the beginning — he who emptied himself of them — and there was never any " not being " for Christ, the Son of God.

This, too, is underscored in the Gospels, and is specifically stated in John 1:1-14. As we read the accounts of his life, what he was from all eternity flashes through in signs so enigmatic that not a soul, not even the disciples, perceived their meaning. In reading the Gospels one has the impression of reading of a poor man of Nazareth who embarked on a prophetic career; but also, as one reads, from time to time there come lightning flashes that make him look different from the poor man that is depicted. These may be such things as the miracles, or the sayings that reveal a wisdom to which flesh and blood could not attain, or the fatefulness of events that on the surface appear commonplace. And yet while we look with awe the impression vanishes, and we find ourselves again gazing simply at the carpenter of Galilee with so unpromising a future.

God, we have said, was never absent from him; nor was he separated from his Father. " I and the Father are one," he says. (John 10:30.) These awesome signs of glory, even in his weakness and self-humiliation, are God breaking through for a moment to illumine what a One this is. In his self-imposed limitations, God in the person of Christ will not be altogether hidden. Thus power and knowledge beyond the ordinary are displayed, not long enough to convince men that God has come upon them, but long and often enough to make them uneasy in the presence of this man. These are the testimonies, not as yet understood but only grasped after the resurrection, to the fact that the poor man of Nazareth was more than he seemed to be. Therefore, we see Jesus in this humility and weakness and suffering and death, irradiated *by a power and a knowledge* not of this world. Hence, his humanity and divinity stand together: humanity such as ours, containing the secrets of God himself.

Power . . . in Weakness

But something that cuts deeper yet remains to be said on this subject. It is not simply in the momentary flashes of power and knowledge, lying beyond human comprehension, that Jesus' divinity is revealed. On the contrary, as was said of the miracles in the last chapter, these flashes are only *signs* of what Jesus was. Where his divinity was most amply revealed was in his Passion and death, together with the many marks of suffering humanity that preceded the last events. As Paul said of himself, Jesus' strength was made perfect in weakness.

It was in the emptying of self, in the sheer ingloriousness of his highly unsuccessful career on earth, that God showed himself perfectly present in Jesus. *We* think of power in purely worldly terms. We think of it as the capacity for achieving earthly goals. This manner of thinking is overthrown by Jesus. He won by losing. He conquered through being the victim of petty religious and political plots. He lived eternally through dying.

This is the all-important aspect of the power of Christ. He emptied himself — and therefore God has exalted him. The flashes of manifest power and transcendent knowledge serve to point out who this Jesus is who stands before us above all *in his weakness*. For him to be *so human* was the true and absolute expression of his *divinity*. Thus we need not concern ourselves as though these terms made for some impossible contradiction. We do not have to solve the mystery of how God could be limited, or how a man could be God. We only have to contemplate what we discern: namely, that God is most evident and precious to faith in the limitations (whether of power or knowledge) that Jesus accepted, and that this man is exalted as Lord of all because he did not strain to show how divine he was. To be despised and rejected was the singular mark of his being God Almighty.

Problem Two: Did Jesus Change?

Closely akin to the questions we have been considering is another problem we undertook to examine — namely, whether Jesus, in his days on earth, went through various stages of development. Anyone, of course, would concede that he had a purely *physical* development from infancy to maturity. But was there any change in outlook, any development in his mind and spirit, any kind of painful pilgrimage through life? Or did he at the time of baptism, or during the temptation in the wilderness, clearly foresee the whole path marked out for him? On the other hand, did he, perhaps, in those earlier days entertain real hopes of being recognized and accepted, though with a consciousness of ominous hazards ahead? To go back still farther, did he from early childhood know who he was and what he was destined to become? When, at twelve years of age, he argued with the scholars in the Temple, was he in full possession of his powers?

Students of the Gospels have sometimes professed to find various phases in Jesus' ministry. They have noted, for example, that after hostility began to mount, he increasingly taught in parables. They have pointed out the landmark that is to be found in Peter's brief confession of Jesus as Messiah. They have pointed out how there came a time when he must make the decision to go to Jerusalem for his last fatal visit.

There is no conclusive evidence in the Gospels as to how Jesus' work on earth unfolded, and therefore, no conclusive evidence as to whether there was any development (implying change) within himself. We cannot be sure why the four writers made their particular and varying selections of material, and fixed the order of events in Jesus' life as each one did. In other words, there is no such thing as a "scientific" biography of Jesus in the modern sense, and certainly no proof as to what was going on in Jesus' mind.

In view, however, of the discussion earlier in this chapter, there is no reason to be disconcerted by the thought that there may have been a development in Jesus, even after he began his public ministry. For if he was truly human, it could be expected that he would live from day to day, and change his opinions according to the shifting of events and the maturing of his mind, and even in the light of those facts alter his initial course of action. This would not be inconsistent with holding that at every stage in his development God was in him, directing his steps. Obedience to his Father's will would doubtless mean obeying in the light of circumstances, rather than by a supernatural prearrangement of every event. But it would nevertheless be the will of the Father that prevailed all along the line. Herein lies the divinity that gave his life order and meaning.

These reflections need cause us no intellectual or theological trouble. What matters is that Jesus faced every situation with no mistake in judgment, and infallibly charted his course as he went along. What matters is that Jesus, in subjecting himself to the human life he chose, *unerringly followed the road of self-denial*. His character as the Son of God is thus evident at every point — the One who emptied himself, that God might be perfectly manifested. This consistency in the Gospel story is apparent even at the most superficial reading. Whether hopes and fears alternated within him is beside the point. How he acted, what he said, what he allowed to happen to him — all this holds together because of what Jesus consistently was and did, and needs no artificial arguments from us to make the pattern constant.

Here we see clearly the difference between Jesus and ourselves. For with us the development of our life involves in-
consistency, errors and new beginnings, repentance and re-
newal, changes of mind, a mixture of false starts and successful
enterprises. It is characteristic of our human nature that it
should be so, and we cannot conceive our life without these
variable and shifting elements. But Jesus Christ, God in human
flesh, was another kind of man. He presents the unique example of human nature being all along what God desired and
flowering as God intended. In Jesus it is revealed what man
can be. He is the New Man, and therefore different. As for
the rest of us, " it does not yet appear what we shall be, but
we know that when he appears we shall be like him, for we
shall see him as he is " (I John 3:2).

Problem Three: Jesus' Sinlessness

There remains yet another specific problem to consider —
namely, whether Jesus as God could have any part in human
sin, or whether, if he was a man, he could deviate so far from
human nature as to be sinless. Once again, though in regard
to a somewhat different kind of issue, we are plunged into the
question of how we are to think of Jesus as both God and
man at the same time — particularly when God and man are
poles apart so far as sinlessness and sinfulness are concerned.

Now in view of the estimate that even non-Christians put
on Jesus' character, there would not at first glance appear to be
much of a problem here. And certainly few persons within the
Christian tradition have ever alleged that he had any fault. It
is well to remember, however, that at this point we are often
governed by sentiment rather than by strict logic. Our thinking is, in fact, apt to become a little careless when we reflect
on the sinlessness of Christ. It seems to be taken for granted

that human goodness lies within the boundaries of human power: that a man can be good, and perhaps even absolutely good, by the exercise of his own will. Thus there would appear to be nothing supernatural about Jesus' goodness. Clearly, however, the New Testament saw more substance in Jesus' perfection than would be indicated by our nods of approval.

It is very remarkable that in the Gospel accounts of Jesus' life and sayings he nowhere expresses (with one ambiguous exception to be noted in a moment) any misgivings in regard to his own righteousness. Yet one gets no impression of what we call *self*-righteousness when anyone else is so uncritical of himself. He speaks strong words of judgment applying to others. He forgives the sins of others. At no point does he confess any sense of guilt or inadequacy. He does not take his own words of warning as applying to himself; nor does he indicate that in any respect he needs forgiveness from either God or man. This, therefore, is the most striking example of being human and yet not partaking of the universal characteristic of humanity — its sinfulness. The writer of The Letter to the Hebrews said a great deal in few words when he wrote that Jesus " in every respect has been tempted as we are, yet without sinning " (Heb. 4:15).

The Problem Within the Problem

There is one saying of our Lord — and only one — that can possibly be used to counteract this general impression that he was without consciousness of sin. It is found in the first three Gospels. Luke and Mark report it in almost identical words. To take Luke's version, a ruler approached Jesus and said: " Good Teacher, what shall I do to inherit eternal life? " Jesus' reply was: " Why do you call me good? No one is good but God alone." (Luke 18:18-19; compare Mark 10:17-18.)

There are similar words in the King James Version of Matt. 19:16-17. But in the Revised Standard Version of the passage in Matthew, Jesus says: "Why do you ask me about what is good?" But this does not relieve us of the need to ponder what is reported in Mark and Luke.

Many ingenious explanations have been offered for this difficult passage. Sometimes it has been treated as an instance of Jesus' rebuking someone who came with mere words of flattery. Extending this thought a little, it has been further suggested that Jesus meant to imply that the inquirer did not realize what he was saying in his glib form of address, and that he should either realize that Jesus was God or else abstain from calling him "good." For all we can definitely know, these may be correct interpretations. It should be noted, however, that the real subject of the narrative from which this passage is taken is not a question about Jesus' divinity but a question asked by a young man who desired to do something to earn eternal life. The question of what we are to understand about Jesus is not the point.

In any event, this one enigmatic saying which no one can profess to interpret infallibly can hardly withstand the weight of evidence that Jesus did not display any sense of sin. In this respect he is singularly unlike all the prophets, poets, and apostles whose words are recorded in Holy Writ, not to mention the saints and martyrs in every age since the coming of Christ. At this point Jesus stands apart.

The Spotless Lamb of Sacrifice

New Testament writers make much of the fact that a Lamb without blemish was slain for the redemption of the world. This turn of speech is, of course, picked up from the Jewish custom of offering up unblemished lambs in sacrifice to God.

In the New Testament, this custom is abolished because Jesus is understood as the spotless lamb, whose self-sacrifice brings salvation to mankind.

Thus the whole doctrine of the atonement depends on the assumption of Jesus' sinlessness. He is to be regarded as the spotless Lamb, whose giving up of self makes sufficient atonement for sin. As Paul puts it, God made Jesus " to be sin who knew no sin, so that in him we might become the righteousness of God " (II Cor. 5:21).

This is the crux of the whole matter. Jesus' sinlessness is not something that we can discuss abstractly, as though we were called upon to pass judgment on our Lord. His sinlessness is not simply a case of personal virtue beyond parallel. What matters for us is not what we think about the character of Jesus, but *what he did* as the righteous One of God who took upon himself the judgment and penalty of sin.

The meaning of Jesus' sinlessness thus cannot be seen merely by reviewing what we know of the facts of his life, and then coming to some conclusion about what kind of man he was. The significance of his sinlessness can perhaps be expressed in a twofold way:

1. Jesus, as a man, became one of us. Though he was without sin in the eyes of God or of himself, he chose to suffer as the rest of us deserve to suffer. This would not be effective for the forgiveness of others if he had not been sinless. In the end he used this record, this achievement, to take lovingly upon himself all our own well-merited burdens. God can forgive *us* because of what *Jesus* was in the name of the human race.

2. Furthermore, Jesus in life and death lived as no other man ever lived. He lived as the New Man — truly human, but redeeming the human race because his goodness broke the old pattern of life and covered up the sins of his fellow men. Here we see again the *interruption* of the sorry history of humanity

by the life, death, and resurrection of One who was human and yet different from ourselves. Because humanity could become, in Jesus, different from what it ever was before or since, we are invited to hope that the future will turn out differently for us from what would have been the case had there been no Jesus Christ.

We must carry our thought still farther. The term " sinlessness," as used in the way the problem was presented, is negative. We need a more positive and dynamic way of thinking. We must think, not so much of the absence of sin, as of the *righteousness* of Christ. This was exhibited in becoming nothing for ourselves, so that the righteousness of God might be revealed — not so much in open acts of power that anyone could recognize, but in love that was not appreciated. Love is the very character of God the Father, and it was equally the character of his incarnate Son. The divine-human nature of Christ is not so much expressed by the mention of his sinlessness as by the thought of his self-emptying in order to make goodness and love triumphant.

In Jesus we discover the outgoing love of God. From the Father it came: in his Son it was perfectly expressed. Its power is such as to do more for us than we know how to ask or think. This is the sinlessness, the righteousness, the love of Jesus, about which no questions are asked when we see its glory and its sovereign might.

4

THE KINGDOM OF GOD

In one respect, the subject of this chapter is unique among the topics discussed in the book as a whole. The other subjects are " barriers to belief " for many of us, because they seem to present obvious and severe intellectual problems that have to be surmounted. Our instinctive feeling is that we cannot begin to understand the miracles, or the divinity of Jesus, not to mention heaven, hell, or predestination.

Here, on the contrary, we are turning to a subject that we perhaps feel that we understand very well indeed. So familiar is the expression " the Kingdom of God," and so commonly is it used, that the *real* barrier to belief in this case is the illusion that we know what we are talking about when we employ the phrase. We have failed to see what immense problems are involved in grasping what the New Testament means when it speaks of " the Kingdom of God." Actually this is a very elusive phrase, used enigmatically in the Bible. Pause long enough to ask yourself: " How would *I* define the Kingdom of God? " Or, to put it in the Bible's own terms, ask yourself: " Precisely what did John the Baptist and Jesus mean by saying, when they announced the start of Jesus' ministry, that the Kingdom was ' at hand '? How would I put this in my own words? "

Confused Without Knowing It

If we are under the impression that it is really quite easy to understand what the Kingdom of God is, the reasons for this impression are not far to seek. During the nineteenth century, as more and more Christians became disturbed about the kind of world they lived in, and anxious to make a better one, the term "Kingdom of God" came into widespread use as a way of referring to the ideal state of affairs toward which the church should strive. Nor was "the Kingdom of God" merely a popular phrase to be incorporated almost automatically into young people's hymns and prayers. It was picked up and developed by learned and responsible theologians in both Europe and America, but in a way that hardly answered to what was in the Bible. The idea of "the Kingdom" became, in many circles, the vogue of the day.

This rather generalized use of the expression was given extra impetus around the turn of the century. For at this time many people in the church were turning their attention, more aggressively than ever, to the *social* ills that plagued mankind — slums, war, poverty, disease. Many concluded that the principal task of the church was to rectify what was wrong in the social order. This emphasis, which came to be called the "social gospel," contrasted sharply with the conventional insistence that Christianity was "concerned with the individual."

In the fertile soil of "the social gospel," the term "Kingdom of God" seemed to grow to new stature. For the aspirations, resolves, hopes, and ideals of humanity were conveniently summed up by referring to the Kingdom of God. The expression became a kind of watchword for social-minded Christians — a watchword that persists to this day.

It would be an interesting, if somewhat exacting, exercise to try to provide a definition of what "the Kingdom of God" was really taken to mean during the era of great aspirations. What is most significant is that it did not (and does not) as a rule signify any precise ideas, but rather an *attitude*. This attitude is illustrated in the very popular phrase — "building the Kingdom of God." But taken as a series of words intended to convey a thought, this phrase does not even make sense. For a kingdom is by definition a realm over which someone rules. If anyone were to "build" the Kingdom of God, it would obviously be the place of God to do so, since it is his Kingdom. Even at that, the verb "build" does not seem especially suitable. A sovereign establishes a kingdom, or conquers one, or carves one out, or reigns over one; he scarcely "builds" one. The word would appear to represent a mixed metaphor, confusing a term borrowed from architecture or mechanics with one taken from political science. In any event, the point of the phrase was not that God did the building, but that man was expected to do so. Thus we have had the anomalous picture of *man* creating *God's* Kingdom.

Much of the importance of this expression lies precisely in its odd and anomalous character. It reflected an unawareness that the Kingdom of God was something that God took care of, and that by no stretch of the imagination could it be considered the result of human effort. Yet the expression also reflected a determination to forget about theological fine points or even accurate language, and get on with the job of making a better world. The concern of those who have most earnestly used this phrase was ethical, social, and political. Their concern was for righteousness on earth. And quite correctly they supposed that how men thought, spoke, and acted had something to do with righteousness.

We cannot, therefore, be contemptuous of even so curious a slogan as "building the Kingdom of God on earth." Anyone who cares about justice, compassion, kindness, good will, and all the other things that matter in a Christian's standard of values, can hardly help feeling a little homesick for the early vigor of " the social gospel." There was a daring, an abandon, a passionate self-spending, that atoned for a great deal of inexact theological language. There was a simple and often sacrificial yearning for righteousness which has made a permanent mark on the life of the church and the life of the nation. As we shall see, these qualities are far from alien to what the Bible means by the Kingdom of God.

Nevertheless, the fact remains that as a watchword, the expression " the Kingdom of God " was used, with little understanding of what it was intended to mean. Such carelessness might be forgiven in a time when the zeal for social righteousness was fighting for its very life. But now that so much of the original zeal has waned, one can hardly excuse looseness of language on the assumption that the church is too fiercely consumed with social action to be worried about its words. Perhaps if we were better informed as to what is really meant by the Kingdom of God, we could more effectively direct our energies, not as would-be builders, but as servants of the Kingdom.

The Enigma of the Kingdom

It is not too surprising if we are unable to define the Kingdom of God — either as we mean it, or as the Bible meant it. For although the expression was very frequently on Jesus' lips, where can we find in the Gospels a definition of the Kingdom?

In Matt. ch. 13, there is a considerable collection of parables about the Kingdom of God. (Matthew uses the phrase " the Kingdom of Heaven " rather than " the Kingdom of God," but the two expressions mean the same thing.) We might expect that in this abundance of material, from Christ's own mouth,

a definition could be discovered. But if so, the definition must
be framed by us. For Jesus himself does not define. He tells
parables, which are comparisons rather than exact descriptions.
What comparisons, then, do we find?

We note that Jesus likens the Kingdom of Heaven, or of
God, to a great variety of things. He says it is as a man who
sowed good seed; but while he slept, an enemy came and sowed
weeds in the same field. (Vs. 24-30.) Then he compares it to a
mustard seed, the smallest of seeds, that becomes a great tree.
(Vs. 31-32.) The Kingdom of Heaven, he says, is like leaven in
bread (v. 33); like treasure hidden in a field, accidentally discovered by someone who sells all his possessions to acquire that
field (v. 44); like a merchant finding a pearl of great price
(vs. 45-46); like a net that gathers in all kinds of fish, to be
sorted out according to their worth (vs. 47-50).

Obviously, there is much to be learned about the Kingdom
from this assortment of varied parables. But our purpose in
enumerating them is not to explain each of these teachings. It
is rather to underscore the fact that Jesus does not give a flat
statement of what the Kingdom is. Instead, he confines himself to this series of cryptic hints. Parables are not, as is so often
imagined, mere " sermon illustrations," designed to make a
point clear. This very chapter in Matthew makes clear that
parables are obscure, difficult to fathom, making demands
upon the hearer rather than clearing up his misunderstandings.
(See vs. 10-17, 51-52.) They are a very special form of teaching,
harder to grasp than plain statements of doctrine. Jesus' hear-
ers, therefore, would have to wrestle with all these enigmatic
sayings in order to discover what he was saying to them; nor
was there any guarantee that they would be successful in the
effort.

It would appear that Jesus was deliberately making the subject of the Kingdom difficult rather than easy. What would be

the reason for this? We note that he was speaking to Jews, to whom the Kingdom of God would not seem like a new idea. They had certainly been familiar from childhood with the belief that God was the King above all kings, that Israel was his kingdom, and that through Israel he intended to reign over all the world. They were acquainted with the thought of God's absolute sovereignty. All they asked was that God *show himself* as king of all the earth: that he hide himself no longer, but step forth in his true colors as ruler of the universe. They were looking, furthermore, for a specially anointed representative of God, the Messiah, and wondered only that he delayed so long in coming. They knew about the Kingdom of God — the Kingdom of God was the very thing they were waiting for.

This being the case, it seems evident that Jesus was intentionally challenging them — not through misleading or inaccurate parables of the Kingdom, but through parables that in some disturbing fashion cut across and contradicted their traditional ideas of what the Kingdom of God really was. Nothing was as simple as they thought it was — least of all the Kingdom of God. If he had come preaching that the Kingdom of God consisted, for example, in obeying all the traditional laws, they could have understood that very easily. Indeed, they could well have mistaken Jesus for just another Pharisee, for the Pharisees thought of the Kingdom somewhat in this way. Or if he had proclaimed that the Roman Empire was soon to be overthrown by a power from on high, that too would have been intelligible, and would have corresponded to what many of them hoped for and believed. But in place of straightforward teachings that anyone could lay hold of, he insisted on his cryptic parables, which not even his own disciples understood. Never would he commit himself to a "doctrine" of the Kingdom. "All this Jesus said to the crowds in parables; indeed he said nothing to them without a parable." (V. 34.)

What does this mean, then, for our understanding of the parables of the Kingdom? The parables, like the miracles, were *signs*—signs pointing on to something not yet perceived. They signified something hidden. In this case, they were designed to suggest many things about the Kingdom that were not obvious. Above all, they were intended to suggest that the Kingdom itself was hidden from sight, and yet present and all-powerful. The conclusion to the chapter we have been examining gives us the clue to what Jesus had been talking about in his parables of the Kingdom. In the concluding verses, and in what appears to be a new episode (vs. 53-58), Matthew records that when Jesus came to his own country, he taught in the synagogue and was rejected. The people angrily or contemptuously asked where "the carpenter's son" got "this wisdom and these mighty works." Finally, Jesus said, "A prophet is not without honor except in his own country and in his own house." And Matthew ends the chapter by saying, "And he did not do many mighty works there, because of their unbelief."

Here is the key to the parables of the Kingdom. Jesus had been speaking all along of himself and his own work — not about an abstract idea of the Kingdom of God. *He* was the treasure hidden in the field, the pearl of great price, the leaven in the loaf, the little mustard seed that grew into a mighty tree. Belief or unbelief in him was what made the difference between the fish that were acceptable and those which were thrown away. The coming of Jesus was the good seed sown in a field, which an "enemy" tried to corrupt.

All these parables have a highly personal reference. What was hidden from the eyes of his contemporaries was that *in Jesus,* the despised and rejected one, the Kingdom of God was present in glory and power. Jesus himself is the secret of the Kingdom.

Four Points About the Kingdom

Let us expand this clue that we have discovered.

In a chapter as brief as this it is naturally impossible to say all that must be said about the New Testament teaching concerning the Kingdom of God. In four points we may, however, hope to summarize some of the essential elements in this teaching.

Point One: The Kingdom has come in Jesus of Nazareth. Jesus himself embodies the Kingdom of God. Here we should note that the very word "kingdom" is probably misleading in the English language, and we preserve it chiefly because of its familiarity. It seems to imply an area, a realm that can be considered in terms of the space it occupies. (Compare our common expression "*extend* the Kingdom of God on earth.") The personalized word "kingship" would serve better. Or we could speak of the royal rule of God — God actually reigning, God in reality establishing his sovereignty.

In Jesus we find God establishing himself with kingly might. But it is a kingly might hidden from the casual gaze. It is not at all evident that this poor and humiliated man Jesus, who stands before us in his weakness, is the very expression of the power and glory of God. Thus, as we have noted in connection with Jesus' parables of the Kingdom, the Kingdom never becomes obvious, never becomes something that we can talk about as though we really understood it. It always eludes our own ideas and expectations. God is King *in his own distinctive way* — incarnation in Jesus of Nazareth. Such a kingship was totally unexpected to Jews and Gentiles alike, who looked for their God (or their gods) to be manifested in a blaze of power that no one could fail to recognize. God was present in Jesus, and men knew it not.

In the light of these comments, it is in order to take a fresh look at the opening words of the preaching of both John the Baptist and Jesus as reported in Matthew. John the Baptist, we are told, came preaching, "Repent, for the kingdom of heaven is at hand" (Matt. 3:2). Jesus, according to ch. 4:17, began his ministry with the same words.

Of what was John the Baptist really speaking? Many imagined that the day of revolution had arrived, that Israel would be restored and magnified, that national and religious greatness were about to materialize once more as of old. But John the Baptist was speaking of a *person:* "I baptize you with water for repentance, but he who is coming after me is mightier than I, whose sandals I am not worthy to carry." (Ch. 3:11.) In Jesus' mouth the same words had a somewhat different force. John had been speaking as the herald of the King. Jesus announced himself, not explicitly, but by every word and act implicitly affirming that he was indeed the One previously heralded, and that his words and deeds constituted the great event so long desired.

As is reported in Luke, for example, there soon came a day when Jesus went to the synagogue at Nazareth, read what Isaiah had to say of the Servant of God, and then declared: "Today this scripture has been fulfilled in your hearing." (Luke 4:21.) The people were furious. They began to suspect that he really meant what he said. Worse than that, what he implied was even more radical than what he expressly stated. The realization that Jesus *actually believed* that he embodied the very presence and kingship of God, led good, pious people to demand his death as a blasphemer. He had never been talking about a kingdom in general: he had all along been testifying to himself. "The kingdom of God is at hand," he had begun by saying. And toward the end he told the Pharisees, "The kingdom of God is not coming with signs to be observed " — that is to say, not in the external, obvious signs they would naturally look for in connection with so great an event. "For behold," he went on, "the kingdom of God is *in the midst of you*" — present already, without their knowing it! (Ch. 17:20-21.)

Point Two: The Kingdom is expressed gloriously and triumphantly in the cross. It is to John, the author of the Fourth Gospel (John does not use the expression "Kingdom of God" at all), that we owe our clearest insight into the nature of the glory and power of the Kingdom. Even as early as in the account of John the Baptist's preaching, the Fourth Gospel gives us a striking statement of what it means for the "kingship" of God to be present and victorious in Jesus. Whereas the first three Gospels report John as saying that the Kingdom was at hand, the Fourth Gospel omits this saying and gives us instead these words from the Baptist: "Behold, the Lamb of God, who takes away the sin of the world! " (John 1:29.) The glory of which John the Baptist testifies is the glory of *sacrifice*.

Throughout the Fourth Gospel there is much about glory; but it is the glory of self-denial, suffering, and death. The hour of glory, according to Jesus, as reported in this Gospel, *is precisely the same as the hour of his death*. This is the way, the wholly unexpected way, conceived only in the divine imagination, by which God establishes his royal rule. In ch. 12:27-33, Jesus questions whether he should pray to be saved from the fatal hour, and then says: "No, for this purpose I have come to this hour. Father, glorify thy name." And a moment later he declares, "Now is the judgment of this world, now shall the ruler of this world be cast out; and I, when I am lifted up from the earth, will draw all men to myself." This, we are told, he said " to show by what death he was to die." The cross will be his throne in the most literal sense. From there he will *rule*. In his final prayer before his arrest, Jesus said, " Father, the hour has come; glorify thy Son that the Son may glorify thee " (ch. 17:1).

As the sacrificial Lamb of God, Jesus reigns as glorious King. The Kingdom of God is completely present in the cross, where Jesus is forsaken, mocked, and ushered into death. This is the victory that overcomes the world.

Point Three: The Kingdom of God is manifested to the few in the resurrection. If victory is already complete in the cross, the resurrection is not to be understood as a triumph following a tragedy. Rather, it is the showing forth of the victory, once and for all, that had already been gained by Jesus' sacrifice of himself upon the cross. To the disciples was given the privilege of learning, at Easter, what they had failed to grasp before, and what they had believed least of all on Good Friday: namely, that Jesus the victim was thereby Jesus the Victor.

It is important to note that the first Easter was not a conspicuous event in its day. Apparently it passed almost unnoticed, apart from the rulers who found that the body of Jesus was no longer in the tomb, and apart from the disciples who were slow to believe what they saw with their own eyes. Thus even the showing forth of Jesus' victory over sin and death was *hidden*. If the intention had been to astound the world by rising from the dead, the event could have been arranged much more sensationally. But this would have been a denial of the very nature of the victory, which achieved life in losing it. Belief in the resurrection thus became a matter for faith, not a fact within the realm of straightforward human knowledge. Hence the importance of Jesus' words to Thomas: " Blessed are those who have not seen and yet believe." (Ch. 20:29.) Once again we see that the Kingdom comes not " by observation." The rule of God was revealed without any fanfare whatsoever. The Kingdom of God was manifested quietly, in an out-of-the-way place, to a few obscure persons.

*Point Four: In the end the Kingdom of God will be mani-
fested to all.* The Bible, nevertheless, does not end its testimony
with the account of the cross and resurrection. It looks for
other events to come, at the conclusion of all history. These
events will not add anything to the glory and triumph of Jesus
on the cross, which is complete and which completely expresses
the Kingdom of God. Sacrifice and self-denial are not just
signs pointing toward the coming Kingdom: they are already
the *full expression* of God's power, which is a power not of
this world.

However, just as the few saw the glory of the cross when
Easter dawned, so everyone will eventually see it. Then everyone will know how strong love is — as strong as death — in
the resurrection of the dead, in the restoring of all that has
been lost in the tragedies of life, in new bodies, in sight for
the blind and hearing for the deaf, above all, in such knowledge of God as we cannot in this world possess. This is the
ultimate *joy* of the Kingdom which is indeed the pearl of
great price, the treasure hidden in a field, the seed that grew
into a towering tree. At *that* point — the end of all history, the
winding up of life as we know it upon earth — *the Kingdom
will no longer be hidden.* What Christ was and is, will be revealed to all: to the sorrow of some, perhaps, but for the re-
newal and remaking of God's whole creation.

The Commandments of the Kingdom

What we have been describing is not to be viewed, however,
just as a stupendous drama played out on a cosmic stage. The
victory which came and will be more generally manifested *had
to do with real righteousness,* not just with a great idea. Referring once again to the preaching of John the Baptist (this
time, as recorded in Luke 3:7-14), we note that in announcing

the coming of the Kingdom, he had very specific things to say to various kinds of people who came to him. He was very serious when he summoned men to repent, for in the face of the oncoming righteousness of God, to be revealed in Jesus, there was an urgency about turning away from sin. John the Baptist had candid words for the complacent (vs. 7-9), strong counsel about works of compassion (vs. 10–11), and concrete advice for tax collectors and Roman soldiers (vs. 12-14).

Jesus was certainly no less specific in his ethical teachings. He laid hard commandments upon all, and most immediately upon his disciples. They too were to find life by losing it. They too were to take up their cross and be victorious in their sufferings and frustrations. In the last parable he told (Matt. 25:31-46), he made it painfully clear that at the day of final decisions the sheep and the goats would be divided because of acts of love done or neglected.

In view of so many strong and even alarming utterances, we obviously have to do more than merely think clearly about theological terms. People do not enter the Kingdom of God simply on the basis of precise thinking. Many, who have been quite inexact in their way of expressing themselves, have done greater things than they knew. Self-denial and sacrifice — the blood-red colors of God's royal victory — have marked many who did not know technically what the Bible meant by the Kingdom of God, as well as many who did. And while the technical knowledge is very much to the point, and gives a greater weight to the whole concept of the Kingdom than careless speech about "building the Kingdom," the very hiddenness of the Kingdom, so often referred to in these pages, is illustrated by many a life of self-giving that is poorly instructed in theology.

For the Kingdom of God means, for all practical purposes, simply this: to be committed to Jesus Christ and to take his commandments seriously. It means to submit to his will; to let him prevail over our own contrary passions, ambitions, and desires. The rule of God becomes personalized, not only in what Jesus did in his own lifetime, but in what he does *in us*. This is Christ acting and reigning now. We do not need to "build" his Kingdom. We *do* need to let him establish his kingship in and through ourselves. Where that happens, and it may have to happen sacrificially, the power and glory of God are once more displayed, however hiddenly.

It thus behooves us at all times to take note of what Christ's kingly rule demands of us. We are summoned to reconsider our ways, and likewise the ways of the world. There is no refuge in the mere contemplation of what Christ is or what he has accomplished: for if we truly contemplate him, we shall find ourselves met with stern commands to take up our cross just where it will matter most to others and will help them most at our expense. When we flee to him for security, he sends us back into the insecurity of the world.

To be subjects of *this* King means to obey, to act, to be sensitive, to be imaginative and resourceful. Above all, it means to be concrete in both what we do and what we shun in his name. The Kingdom of God breaks in upon us to interrupt our self-centered existence, and forces us to look out of our private worlds upon the world at large where the harvest is great and the laborers are few. The Kingdom of God challenges our lovelessness, our hardness, our self-seeking. It challenges us by the awful judgment passed upon us by the meekness and the pity of Jesus Christ. It challenges us by the compassion of him who gave his own earthly life that others might have what he did not enjoy. It challenges us by the triumph in life and death which only gentleness could win.

HEAVEN AND HELL

It is human nature to want to consign Hitler and Stalin to hell. Likewise, it is human nature to suppose that the best person we ever knew will go to heaven. For *punishment* and *reward* loom large in our ways of thinking, and we are quick to believe that rogues are eternally punished and the good perpetually rewarded. Whether or not we take literally the Bible's descriptions of heaven and hell — streets of gold versus fires that burn forever — we certainly cling to the idea that there is a vast difference between the hope of saints and the doom of sinners.

Wrong Approaches

Teachings about heaven and hell have often been a problem to faith because of the Bible's vivid imagery. Heaven and hell have been spoken of traditionally as though they were specific regions, which could be located on a cosmic map. Furthermore, the way in which eternal bliss and everlasting perdition are usually thought of seems more suitable to ancient thinking than to the modern mind. Finally, the love of God seems to have no place in the literal interpretation of what hell is. Why would the God who gave his Son for the world's salvation will that any man should burn forever?

Yet these are not the really basic problems that beset us in this subject. We have learned enough about the Bible's way of speaking to understand that much of its language is deliberately figurative. Nor are we, after all, too seriously pressed by the question of whether heaven and hell are areas with definite geographical boundaries. Even the apparent contradiction between the love of God and the eternal fire is not what needs to concern us most of all. For the fact is that whether or not God desires the death of a sinner, *we* do. If Scripture said nothing at all about heaven and hell, we would undoubtedly still retain our convictions that eternity will not be the same for every man, or at any rate ought not to be so. We would insist on reward and punishment for humanity, because men differ so much in character that we cannot conceive how all can be treated alike.

The Demand for Justice

There are, however, many problems attached to the simple view of life that call for appropriate punishment or reward for everyone. For one thing, most people cannot easily be classed among either the wicked or the righteous. Even such distinguished servants of Christ as Luther, Calvin, and Knox undeniably had grievous faults. Even those whom we most admire among our friends, relatives, and contemporaries are, we must reluctantly confess, not without blemish. As for ourselves, the less said the better. If everyone is destined for either punishment or reward, it is a puzzle to know how the proper people are to attain paradise. Nobody deserves it. Or, if we incline to judge people severely, we shall be forced to wonder what God thinks of the limited good points that can be credited to almost anybody.

This is why the Roman Catholic doctrine of purgatory is so convenient. Roman Catholicism recognizes that strictly on the basis of merit few persons are so evil that hell is inevitable, and also that few are so saintly that there is no impediment to their entrance into heavenly reward. Therefore, Roman Catholic dogma sets up the doctrine of an intermediate state. Most persons, according to this doctrine, are fated to endure long ages of torment to purge their souls, and at length to be so purified as to be entitled to enjoy heavenly bliss. It is a handy doctrine to account for what happens to the majority of people after death, but unfortunately it has no basis in Scripture. It has been manufactured out of whole cloth.

In any event, the idea of purgatory has little appeal to Protestants. At the same time, we have few or no constructive ideas of our own about what course divine justice ought to take in dealing with that mixture of favorable and unfavorable points that goes into the record of every individual. Of one thing we feel sure, however, as an instinctive reaction to life: reward and punishment ought to be the lot of people according to their worth.

To be sure, there is much vindictiveness, mixed with an equal amount of favoritism, in this instinctive feeling. It is not, that is to say, exactly a view that we have thoughtfully reasoned out. On the contrary, we usually have some strong sentiments as to who should get what kind of treatment at the divine bar of justice: and these sentiments have had no small influence on our speculations about the fate of men after death. We hardly pause to recollect that according to the Bible it is God, and not man, who makes decisions about individuals.

And yet, for all our subjectivity in this matter, for all our personal animus and personal predilections, we surely are reacting with an elementary sense of justice. It is obvious to us that men are not all of equal virtue or of equal iniquity, and it seems just as obvious that God may be expected to do something about this inequality. This sense of justice, quite aside from explicit teachings of Scripture, keeps some sort of notion of heaven and hell alive in our thinking. We may personally have abandoned the thought of either heaven or hell as a specific *place*. We may, indeed, have found any concept of hell repugnant. Yet what becomes of men in the long run, in the face of God's judgment, is not an issue that can easily be dropped.

We do not rid ourselves of this concern by recollecting that by the very nature of original sin all men are at fault in God's sight; that all have fallen and come short of the glory of God. Nor do we get rid of it by recalling that what the gospel is about is forgiveness, not retribution; and that we know ourselves in the end as standing on level ground with the worst of sinners, having no hope except the grace of God. (Did not Paul call himself " the chief of sinners "?) The feeling still persists that *justice will not be done unless some distinction is made between the best and worst of men.* The record that men make on earth surely cannot be irrelevant to how God at length views them at his judgment seat.

When we turn to the Bible, we find this view immensely strengthened by the teachings of no less an authority than Jesus himself. Again and again he denounced the Pharisees in terms that certainly suggested that they could come to no good end. Indeed, he inquired explicitly how they could escape the damnation of hell (see Matt. 23:33, and the entire chapter). In several of his parables he indicated in no uncertain terms that those who proved to be unworthy or perverse would be punished eternally: for example, see the parable of the unforgiving servant (ch. 18:23-35), of the wheat and the tares (ch. 13:24-43), of the sheep and the goats (ch. 25:31-46). In Mark 9:43-49 there is an eloquent passage, bidding the disciples remove offending members of their bodies — hands, feet, or eyes — rather than be cast whole into the fire that is not quenched. The thought of outer darkness, of weeping and gnashing of frustrated teeth, was often expressed in Jesus' words.

The rest of the New Testament is not less forbidding, and in the book of Revelation damnation comes with vengeance upon cities and peoples who have defied God. Clearly, there is Scriptural reason for looking into these categories of retribution and reward. The grace of God is indeed the theme of the Bible; but there is also too much in it about judgment to warrant our overlooking this threatening element. Nor does it seem possible, even on the basis of forgiveness, to overlook the stress of the Scriptures on the obedience required of us in order that our eternal inheritance may be attained.

The Damnation of Judas Iscariot

It is not possible within this chapter to track down every Scriptural reference to heaven and hell. Perhaps, however, two clues to the whole matter may be found by looking rather closely at two short sayings from the New Testament, neither of which speaks of heaven or hell directly. The first has to do with Judas Iscariot. After he had hanged himself, and his position among the apostles must be taken by another, there is a short but suggestive obituary of Judas, saying that he turned aside from discipleship " to go to his own place " (Acts 1:25).

It can be argued that the phrase " to his own place " is a roundabout way of describing hell. This does not mean that a more polite term has been substituted for a rough one. The writer is not being coy about the word " hell." He was indirectly defining what hell is, in the strictest sense of the word. We are not, therefore, entitled to take some other idea about hell and read it into this verse. We shall be wiser to take this phrase from The Acts, and understand hell in the light of it: hell is where such a one as Judas Iscariot belongs.

To appreciate the full force of this, it is necessary to consider the strange and terrible case of Judas. The fact that we know very little about him has long served as an invitation to speculate about him. A great many theories have been advanced to explain his actions. The view that he simply sold his Lord in order to acquire thirty pieces of silver hardly seems adequate; one would not expect to find such a person at any time among Jesus' disciples. In any event, extreme remorse followed so speedily that one would have to suppose that if Judas for a moment yielded to purely mercenary motives, he was complex and sensitive enough to realize the enormity of his sin. A fairly widespread opinion is that Judas really hoped to force Jesus' hand and compel him to show himself in his true colors as the Messiah. Being dissatisfied with Jesus' conduct as the expected leader of Israel, he thought that a crisis would move him to act dramatically. When this plan failed, Judas was filled with either frustration or remorse, or both, and destroyed himself.

Doubtless on the principle that to know all is to forgive all, theories to explain Judas' act of betrayal have sometimes led theorizers to soften their opinion of the traitor. It has sometimes happened that in the course of explaining his conduct people have made excuses for him and suggested that he was painted in colors far too black; however, this is not necessarily the outcome of the theory mentioned above.

What the true explanation of Judas' behavior is one would be foolish to profess to know. The Bible offers no theories to analyze his psychology, except for John's flat assertion that he was a thief. By the same token, there is nothing in the Bible to justify a mild view of Judas' offense. The striking thing is that this person stands out, in the pages of Scripture, as a symbol of pure evil. He is the man into whom the devil entered, the chosen instrument of Satan to bring about the death of Jesus. He was the traitor in the midst who, at the Last Supper, went out into the night, never to return as a disciple but only as the betrayer. The author of the Fourth Gospel, who makes much of the imagery of light and darkness, stresses that when Judas went out " it was night " (John 13:30). Jesus said that " it would have been better for that man if he had not been born " (Matt. 26:24). What the precise motives were that led Judas on his dark course we shall probably never find out. No good concerning him is mentioned in Scripture. A curse rests on his name. His final obituary is this awful pronouncement — that he might " go to his own place."

Perhaps this obituary tells us all we need to know about Judas, and all we need to know about hell. Judas went to his own place. He went his own way. The other disciples offer a striking comparison. To be sure, during Jesus' lifetime they were frequently dull, quarrelsome, perverse, and unreliable. Rebellious thoughts found expression in their words, most notably when Peter sought to deter Jesus from going to Jerusalem to die. This same Peter committed the offense that, next to Judas' sin, is the most sensational in the Gospels. He denied his Lord. Complete misunderstanding of Jesus and his mission is often reflected in the comments of the disciples. Even after the resurrection Thomas displayed a mood of skepticism, doubt, and unbelief.

Yet none of these others severed himself completely from the influence of his Master. Peter, after having denied his Lord, wept bitterly, and visited his tomb. Crushed though they were by the calamity of Good Friday, the group did not dissolve. They were still searching for the meaning of all that had happened — in despair, yet reasoning among themselves to find the secret of this heartbreaking riddle. Judas, on the other hand,

had made an irrevocable decision that took him out of this
circle " to his own place." Why he did so, we cannot know.
What twisted thoughts and perverted reasoning went on inside his mind, no one can tell. But at all events he followed the
bent of his own nature. He sought and found his own level.
And this turned out in the end to be treachery and self-destruc-
tion, despair without hope, remorse that could find no relief,
a rope and a tree and darkness beyond — the logical ending of
what began badly, the natural harvest of bad seeds. This was
" his own place," the hell of just being himself.

Land of Promise

That is the first clue.

But now we must turn to the second short clue to the enigma
we are studying. It is to be found in a saying of Jesus that he
spoke after Judas had left the room on that fateful night. To the
remaining disciples he said: " I go to prepare a place for you.
And if I go and prepare a place for you, I will come again, and
receive you unto myself; that where I am, there ye may be also."
(John 14:2, 3.) Here was Jesus' comforting word concerning
the hope of heaven. Where the " place " might be, or what it
would be like, he did not say. It was enough that there was a
future for the disciples that was *good* — a future because Christ
had a future, and good because Christ determined it.

This was a word that could not be spoken to Judas. He was
headed toward his own place. The others were, so to speak,
faced toward Christ's place, the place he was preparing for
them, not through any merit of their own, but simply through
what Christ was doing for them. They were due to inherit, not
the natural fruit of their stupidity or perversity, not the harvest
of their weakness and their lust and their self-centeredness, but
the consequences of what Christ was for their sakes. It was

from this inheritance that Judas cut himself off, preferring absolutely to go his own way. It was not asked of Judas that he be a saint. All that was asked was that he, as the rest eventually did, let his own self fall asleep in Jesus, and wait for the reward — the reward not of his life but of Jesus' life and death.

What any one of the disciples was in himself held no great promise. It would not be to the advantage of any of them to come at the end to his own place: that is to say, to go on simply developing along the old lines, to reach the natural conclusion of the life he had been living all along. The disciples' hope was bound up wholly and entirely with the future of Jesus Christ — where *he* was going, what *he* was going to achieve, what was going to become of *him*. Judas, by contrast, preferred to travel his own route and follow his own line, and so his life ripened at last into the harvest that could be expected.

That is the difference between heaven and hell. That is what the whole question is about. Hell is to be understood as the end result of self-determination. Thus there are many signs and premonitions of hell on earth. Individuals and organizations and nations go their own way, and bring down upon their heads and also upon the heads of innocent bystanders the consequences of their having been a law unto themselves. Every today bears its fruits tomorrow. The accumulated self-will of humankind is heaped up, so that instead of progress the world in every age encounters a new visitation of woe. The road that man naturally follows leads from bad to worse. We see this in our present life, and who is to say that on a universal scale there is not a vastly greater kind of reckoning? It is toward such a reckoning that the negative side of Jesus' parables points, and we are not able, therefore, to assert glibly that in the end all men are saved. This sinister side of the New Testament forbids us to relax in the expectation of ultimate and universal salvation. Judas Iscariot stands as the symbol of the *possibility*

that even the grace of Jesus Christ will not in the end prevail
over every man.

Jesus Christ, however, offers to break the unhappy chain of
moral causes and effects. He interposes himself between what
men have been and the consequences of their lives. Because
of what he has been, said, and done, nothing need ever be the
same for them again — in this life or in the world to come. The
gospel is that he has gone to prepare a place for us. It is a place
that is happily not our own place, but *his*.

We call for justice, but the gospel is that, happily for us,
we do not *receive* justice. There will come a time when this is
the last thing we would crave for ourselves. If we will be, in
the long run, so anxious and so glad to escape inexorable justice, and if the gospel holds out the hope that we may have this
blessed escape, we surely ought not to be so exercized as we are
that justice be done to others. The gospel is for them as well
as for us. They too may come to the place that would not
have been anticipated on the ground of all that they had been
in the past. With all humanity we may join in trusting that
nobody among us will end up where he belongs.

The message of the New Testament is that Christ's grace is
very great and able to interrupt the deadly cycle of desires and
sins and consequences. Human self-assertion gives us all the
clue we need as to what hell is. Our clue as to what heaven is
lies in the promise of becoming something different from what
we are, and of entering into a heritage that we could not have
looked for on the basis of all that our life heretofore has been.
Heaven is transformation, a different conclusion from the logical one, a " place " that we have done little or nothing to prepare for ourselves. Faced by judgment, we shall be glad enough
not to have to lie down in the bed we have made for ourselves.
We shall be glad, in the ultimate rendering up of accounts, that
the outcome of all our yesterdays is not what could have been

expected. We shall be glad to escape from ourselves, from the fire of our own self that is not quenched, from the worm of our self-will that does not die. We shall in the end ask above all *not* to go to our own place, but to be received into the place Christ has prepared. We shall desire most of all not to find ourselves where the road of our own choosing would naturally lead us — where Judas is — but to be instead where Jesus is.

Not Judas, but Ourselves

Much has been said in this chapter about Judas Iscariot. It must not be forgotten, however, that out of the twelve disciples, all manifestly unworthy, Judas was the only one whom the Scriptures depict in the darkest possible colors. His presence in the Gospel accounts stands for the possibility of pure evil. His presence stands for the possibility of being cut off from God. Because there was such a man as Judas, it is out of the question to assert an optimistic universalism, which sees all creatures brought at last under the rule of Jesus Christ. At the same time, the eleven other disciples, all so undistinguished by merits of their own, all so human, all so fallible, testify to the power of grace to cover up human sin.

Nothing could be more unsuitable than for us to presume to pass judgment upon men — murderers, dictators, or saints. There is a curtain of privacy that must be drawn around the whole question of judgment. What became of Hitler is not open to our investigation. Indeed, what became of Judas himself is indicated in rather cryptic fashion by the Bible. We have interpreted the phrase " to his own place " as meaning all we can know about hell, and the expression is appallingly suggestive because we can very well guess what it would mean for *us* to go to our own places. Yet even with Judas it is not positively asserted that he was beyond hope. What ultimately happened to him was between Judas and God.

We began this chapter by noting that an elemental sense of justice seems to demand that saints be rewarded and scoundrels punished. Despite a sentimental view of the loving Fatherhood of God, which gives us a distaste for the Bible's imagery in regard to hell, in everyday life we actually do assume that the wicked and the righteous both receive the justice they deserve. More than that, in practical affairs we are disposed to decide who are the sheep and who are the goats. Hell thus becomes, in effect, the fate of those whom we happen to dislike.

If it is impossible to assert anything like universalism, it is equally impossible to assert that anyone is damned — much less to say *who* is damned. It is God's prerogative to make such fateful decisions. Thus no clear-cut and abstract doctrine of divine justice is to be found in the Bible. What we have is a shadow — a formidable shadow — hanging over human life.

Who is under this shadow but ourselves?

We are the people to whom Jesus' words of warning in his parables are addressed. We are the people who have the chance to be compassionate or hard of heart, responsible or irresponsible, pharisaical or understanding. In terms of the two clues pursued in this chapter, we are the people who have the opportunity to follow our natural bent of character, or to let Jesus Christ interrupt the unhappy cycle of our lives with his transforming grace. Heaven and hell are not general considerations, to be debated in respect to others, but highly personal considerations that pertain first and foremost to us who ask if justice will be done — and who will welcome it most gladly if mercy and not judgment is our lot.

As for our beloved categories of thought — punishment and reward — it must be said that reward is for Jesus Christ alone. Merit is not something that we can attribute to human nature as it is, even at its best. The only human merit that in the long run is decisive in God's sight is Jesus' goodness.

We are allowed to share in what he gained by virtue of what he was, and are not compelled to suffer what in our self-determination we have earned. Punishment is best understood as the fruit of all that has preceded. That is to say, if there be eternal " punishment " for any of us, it is because of self-assertion that will not permit Jesus Christ to break in upon us. What is meant, in the Biblical sense, by punishment is not the vindictive act of an angry God. What is meant is rather the unholy and destructive harvest of all we have been. To attain heaven is to share in Jesus' victory over sin and death — that is, his victory over *ourselves*. To go down to hell is to be nothing but our natural selves, cut off from the true God because we have preferred to remain gods of our own making.

The vivid language of the New Testament about hell and heaven does not furnish us exactly with a " doctrine." Such language is intended to provide an ominous shadow and a joyful hope, both to be taken with the utmost seriousness for ourselves. As for the innumerable questions that suggest themselves for speculation — for example, what becomes of the heathen who never heard of Christ, or whether the murderer with time to repent has a better chance of salvation than his victim who was shot down suddenly with no opportunity for repentance — we have no choice but to leave such speculations strictly alone. These matters are none of our business. What is meant by heaven and hell is only known to us when we have the wisdom to believe that grace may gain the one and to hope that we may be spared the other. Any further exploration would take us into unknown and indeed forbidden territory. It is enough to shudder at the thought that we could have been left without grace, and to be thankful for the expectation that, despite ourselves, we may enter into life eternal.

6

PREDESTINATION

Where two or three Presbyterians are gathered together in a Bible class, there is likely to be a discussion of predestination. No subject, it would seem, so much fascinates Presbyterians, who apparently feel an almost parental relationship to this difficult doctrine. Not only is it a favorite topic for consideration among adults, but it is said to be widely debated in "bull sessions" of Presbyterian young people. Many persons, both within and outside the Presbyterian Church, are under the impression that next to the form of government practiced by this church, the most distinctive thing about being a Presbyterian is believing in predestination.

Now when one reads Calvin or the Westminster Confession of Faith, it is very clear why Presbyterianism and predestination have been so closely linked together. Certainly the authorities in the Presbyterian Church have from early times been attached to this doctrine. What is overlooked, however, is that the idea is by no means an invention of Presbyterians, and that Calvin had no monopoly on teaching this doctrine.

Augustine, the church father of an earlier century, was preoccupied with predestination. Luther, in what he had to say about free will, went as far as Calvin. Roman Catholics, too, have the conception of predestination embedded in their church dogma. In fact, their most famous and authoritative theologian, Thomas Aquinas, developed the idea very strongly in his writings. In a much later century, the French Roman Catholic thinker Pascal speculated about this baffling and yet fascinating subject.

It would be difficult to find many branches of the Christian church that have not in one way or another been affected by the question of predestination. Even those who reacted most strongly against Calvin's views, in the centuries following his career, were up in arms against something that they recognized as important. In other words, their reaction was prompted not merely by disagreement with Calvinistic views but by a feeling that a Christian had to come to grips with this subject. Controversy about it has become at times exceedingly lively and has led to extreme opinions on both sides of the fence. Karl Barth, perhaps the greatest theologian to appear since the Reformation, has in our own day attempted to take hold of the question of predestination in a new way, and it remains to be seen what will become of his contributions to this age-old discussion.

Why the Preoccupation?

Stress has been laid upon the number of notable people who have taken predestination very seriously, because the next question is, Why did so many think that it mattered so much? The answer is very simple. Both in the Old Testament and in the New Testament, God is described as being so absolutely sovereign that theologians (which means all of us) have to try to make something out of this aspect of Biblical teaching. The apostle Paul had a number of specific references to predestination, but if this were all there were about the matter in the

Scriptures, we could perhaps handle it without too much difficulty. Actually the Bible is full of material that makes one wonder where the divine will leaves off and the human will is given a chance to assert itself. The word "predestination" as such might not be so important if it did not stand for the whole Biblical stress upon the overruling will of a sovereign God.

In popular thinking, of course, predestination is not usually studied in connection with what the Bible as a whole has to say. On the contrary it has simply been more or less equated with fatalism. It has come to be regarded as a view of life that thinks of all events being ordered and directed by some inevitable force within the universe that is beyond human control. If for "the will of God" we substitute "fate," we have fairly well described the popular notion of predestination. It becomes equivalent to saying that "what must be, must be." Anyone who has been in service has heard the military equivalent: "Somewhere there is a bullet with your number on it."

Nor is this kind of interpretation confined to purely popular thinking. For example, so distinguished a modern historian as Arnold Toynbee, in his famous *A Study of History,* speaks of Calvinism with something like contempt, because of what he understands as the Calvinistic concept of predestination. Describing this belief as "an idolatrous perversion" and a "fatalistic creed," he goes on to liken it first to Islam, then to nineteenth-century ideas of inevitable progress, and at length to Marxist determinism.

Pride, Prejudice, and Predestination

Before looking into the question of whether or not predestination and fatalism are more or less the same thing, there might be some wisdom in pausing to ask why Presbyterians, who have predestination written so large in their creeds, are preoccupied by the subject. Various reasons immediately come to mind.

In the first place, in so far as predestination is regarded as fatalistic, it must be acknowledged that fatalism is indeed fascinating. If I have no control over my own destiny, if all that is to happen to me is really foreordained and inescapable, that becomes a formidable fact of life for me. I cannot be other than absorbed in contemplating the bonds of sheer necessity, determined for me by some power beyond the reach of human effort; for then I am certainly caught in a trap from which I cannot break loose through any amount of trying. At the same time, there is undoubtedly comfort in the thought that my life, here and hereafter, is fully arranged for me. If I believe that I am among the elect, selected for a great destiny, I am undergirded in the stresses and strains of life. Furthermore, this feeling of being among those for whom God has foreordained a great destiny will actually spur me on to bold actions. This has been the case with Calvinists historically, when they took literally their belief that they were set aside for big things. They have been recognized as uncommonly courageous and aggressive in religion, politics, or for that matter in the business transactions of everyday life. Since predestination has been so widely interpreted in this manner in Presbyterian circles, one reason for fascination with a doctrine at one so disturbing and so challenging becomes perfectly obvious.

In all of this there is a certain element of pride. Yet this element of pride is closely associated with a kind of self-consciousness and sensitivity, which also helps to account for why people in general (and Presbyterians in particular) are concerned about this doctrine. For, as conventionally understood, it is a doctrine that is open to obvious attack. If predestination is just determinism in the name of the Lord, Calvinism can be and often has been subjected to severe criticism on the ground that it destroys freedom of will and in fact makes the whole human struggle meaningless. Calvinists have long been aware that they were vulnerable to this sort of attack, and if they enjoy the doctrine it is with an uneasy mind. Perhaps this could be the fatal weakness in Calvin's whole system of thought, as the critics say. Perhaps it really has led to a sort of irrational arrogance that does not stand up to inspection. The reaction of Calvinists to these possibilities has been either to become defensive, and make the doctrine of predestination more rigorous than ever, or else to look for some graceful means of retreat.

Because of this, many Calvinists themselves have wanted to tone down the doctrine. In this they have much in common with a large proportion of Christendom. The Presbyterian Church in the U.S.A., back in 1902–1903, went so far as to add a Declaratory Statement, pertaining to predestination, to the denomination's Confession of Faith. The Presbyterian Confession of Faith, originating in the seventeenth century, had, if possible, gone farther than Calvin himself in building the idea of predestination into the whole system of Presbyterian doctrine. Chapter III of the Confession of Faith is entitled " Of God's Eternal Decree," and it categorically teaches that from all eternity God decreed that some men would be predestined to everlasting life, and others to everlasting death. It is in fact stated that " these angels and men, thus predestined and foreordained, are particularly and unchangeably designed; and their number is so certain and definite that it cannot be either increased or diminished " (Sec. 4). Moreover, this thought of the eternal election of some and the eternal reprobation of others runs as a basic theme throughout large parts of the whole Confession of Faith, not just the controversial Chapter III.

To offset such unqualified avowals, the Declaratory Statement was appended. This Statement, in part, asserts that " the doctrine of God's eternal decree is held in harmony with the doctrine of his love to all mankind, his gift of his Son to be the propitiation for the sins of the whole world, and his readiness to bestow his saving grace on all who seek it." It further asserts that "men are fully responsible for their treatment of God's gracious offer; that his decree hinders no man from accepting that offer."

Whether or not this Declaratory Statement is really logical is not the question to be discussed here. The point to observe is that the rigors of the "eternal decree," arbitrarily made by God with the effect of saving some and damning others, had by 1902–1903 grown repugnant to at least one member of the Reformed or Presbyterian church family. Here we have a deliberate effort to authorize a gentler view of predestination than seems to be taken by the Confession of Faith itself. The "eternal decree" is to be held "in harmony with" a doctrine of divine love that would appear to point in a quite different direction. Despite the phrase "in harmony with," many would see this Declaratory Statement as *contradictory to* the stringent doctrine of predestination traditionally held by Calvinists.

The above developments have been stressed, because it would seem apparent that the time has come when Christians must carefully rethink some of their conventional teachings, and not seek merely to cover their tracks. It is not the role of this book to rewrite the creeds of churches, Calvinistic churches or any others. If that were to be done, it would be the responsibility of duly constituted church authorities. Two things, however, may properly be attempted in these pages. One is to cut through the confusion to indicate what the doctrine of predestination, as taught by the Reformers, was basically trying to affirm. The other is to point out some Biblical insights that considerably relieve the traditional dilemma of predestination versus free will.

Positive Predestination

As to what Calvin and other Reformers were striving to say through their insistence on predestination, the fundamental clue is in the Protestant belief that man is saved by *grace alone*. Man is saved by God's choice, decision, and action. Here once more we come upon the theme that has been stated in this book, and it is this: God intrudes his will, he invades and interrupts our life, by his grace, so that life may turn out differently from what would have been the case had we been left to our natural resources. Predestination means that there is an overruling will, more than the equal of our perverted wills, that turns us toward salvation and away from the natural consequences of what we are. God has predestined us — that is to say, singled us out to receive his mercy, love, and grace instead of the wrath that we deserve. Our destiny (compare the word *predestination*) is to be with God, because he has chosen us to be his beloved people.

Few Protestants would quarrel with these assertions, and it is to the Reformers that we owe the rediscovery of these Biblical teachings. However, Calvin's teaching on predestination has been criticized severely, because besides stressing the grace of God he insisted on being rigorously logical about drawing negative as well as positive conclusions. In other words, along with his basic message that man is saved by grace alone, he inserted the sobering thought that many are *not* chosen for salvation but instead are destined for damnation.

Calvin repeatedly discouraged speculation as to the basis on which God made such a fateful separation between people. This, he said over and over again, lay in the secret counsels of God; and we could only succeed in perturbing ourselves if we were to try to search out the reasons for his giving grace to some and denying it to others. What Calvin felt was remarkable was not that some should be destined to perdition, but that any should receive mercy. In a little book entitled *Instruction in Faith* (intended to inform the lay people of Geneva as to the basic matters of Christian doctrine), Calvin wrote:

"For, if he [God] willed to ruin all mankind, he has the right to do it, and in those whom he rescues from perdition one can contemplate nothing but his sovereign goodness." Where Calvin's interest chiefly lay is revealed in these words that quickly follow in the same book: "What do we seek in election except that we be participants in the life eternal? And we have it in Christ, who was the life since the beginning and who is offered as life to us in order that all those who believe in him may not perish but enjoy the life eternal. If, therefore, in possessing Christ through faith we possess in him likewise life, we need no further inquire beyond the eternal counsel of God."

In respect to the church, Calvin avoided the pitfall of presuming to decide who were the elect and who were the reprobate, and then on that basis determining who should be church members. Firm though he was about church discipline, he did not claim that the "true" church could be set up through discerning those destined for perdition, and then excluding them. That was a sectarian development, which Calvin abhorred. Consistent with his own theory, that the distinction between the saved and the damned lay within God's secret counsels, he taught that God's judgments are far beyond anything we can apprehend. In his largest work, *Institutes of the Christian Religion,* Calvin wrote: "For those who seemed the most abandoned, and were generally considered past all hope, are recalled by his goodness into the right way; while some, who seemed to stand better than others, fall into perdition."

Then, after acknowledging that we need in some measure to know who may be considered God's children, he adds this wise and churchly statement: "And as it was not necessary that on this point we should have an assurance of faith, he [God] has substituted in its place a judgment of charity, according to which we ought to acknowledge as members of the church all those who by a confession of faith, and exemplary life, and a participation of the sacraments, profess the same God and Christ with ourselves." Thus the question of who are the sheep and who are the goats (referred to in the preceding chapter) is ultimately a matter of *God's* decision, and must be left so.

Whether or not Calvin was justified in insisting so vehemently as he did that predestination logically means that if some are saved others are abandoned, may be open to question. As an evangelical minister of Jesus Christ his work was to proclaim the gospel, not to declare the alleged necessity of damnation. But it is also open to question whether or not, in evaluating Calvin's theology, we are justified in singling out this element and judging his whole system of thought in the light of it. For when one reads Calvin thoroughly, with a view to his broad perspective and not just to pick out possibly objectionable factors in what he taught, it is perfectly clear that his intention was to assert our complete dependence upon God's grace. This is the real import even of his intensive treatments of predestination. Not by merit but by grace is any man saved. That is what Luther had taught, and Calvin's message was at heart no different. Predestination, as something willed by God and not earned, signified reliance upon God's sovereign grace. It signified that Christians had known him as a God who reached out to them in love — reached out to those who did not deserve love but were given it anyhow, because "God is love." Without God's will intruding itself for our redemption, we could only come at last to the harvest of all our perversity and sin. But fortunately for us God had the first and last word in the matter. That is the positive meaning of predestination as Calvin taught it. That is the positive meaning of this doctrine for evangelical Christians today.

Predestination Is Freedom

From an intellectual viewpoint, doubtless the most vexing question in this whole matter is the apparent fatalism of the doctrine of predestination. For predestination, however interpreted, seems to leave the human will simply impotent, and to destroy any idea of real freedom or real choice on our part.

Here we come to another modest contribution that this chapter hopes to make to an understanding of what predestination really means. It is a contribution that can be made only by calling close attention to one of the most basic passages in Holy Writ, namely, Rom., ch. 8. This great chapter should serve as our chief guide in realizing what the Bible intends by its teaching about predestination. Given this chapter from Paul, most of what we need to know about the subject falls into place. (The brief synopsis that follows is no substitute for reading the text itself.)

Romans 8:1-8 affirms what we have already said was the principal intent of the Reformers in bringing up the subject at all. "There is therefore now no condemnation for those who are in Christ Jesus," Paul begins. Then he goes on to point out that our sinful flesh is liberated from the necessity of obeying the law of sin and death. This is the good news of the gospel: that men are made free to live as the children of God, to live for God, and to live in obedience to God.

In v. 15, the apostle says to any of us who are led by the Spirit of God: "You did not receive the spirit of slavery to

fall back into fear, but you have received the spirit of sonship."
Here is the thought of freedom once again. We are free to
escape from fear, free to live as sons of God " and fellow heirs
with Christ " — provided we are willing to suffer with Him
who opened this new door of liberty (vs. 16-17).

A little later in the chapter Paul extends his thought of freedom to the whole creation: " The creation itself will be set free
from its bondage to decay and obtain the glorious liberty of
the children of God." (V. 21.)

Still later Paul comes to his famous statement that " we
know that in everything God works for good with those who
love him, who are called according to his purpose " (v. 28).
This is immediately followed by the words: " For those whom
he foreknew he also predestined to be conformed to the image
of his Son, in order that he might be the first-born among
many brethren." (V. 29.) Here predestination is explicitly
mentioned, and in connection with the *good* purpose of God
which seeks the good of his people. No shadow falls across
this positive affirmation.

At v. 31 Paul launches into the famous conclusion of this
chapter, which can be readily identified for the reader by quot-
ing a few phrases: " If God is for us, who is against us? . . .
Who shall bring this charge against God's elect? It is God
who justifies; who is to condemn? . . . Who shall separate
us from the love of Christ? Shall tribulation, or distress, or
persecution, or famine, or nakedness, or peril, or sword? . . .
No, in all these things we are more than conquerors through
him who loved us. . . ."

There is no space for a detailed exposition of the passages
referred to here. None, however, is necessary, in order to bring
out the main point that must be understood as to predestination. It is this: So far from teaching a fatalistic philosophy of
life, Paul resoundingly proclaims that we are given our *liberty*
through what God has willed — over and above anything we

could possibly will for ourselves. This is in the sharpest possible contrast to ancient pagan thought. For in the pagan world of Paul's time it was commonly thought that human beings were in bondage to cosmic powers — be they gods or demons. "Fate," as something whimsical, arbitrary, and inescapable, ruled the universe. The modern counterpart might be called "luck," which is not quite so philosophical an idea. But even in the somewhat more vulgar idea of mere " luck " or " chance " we do have a reflection of *fate* as the controlling fact of life.

As the idea of fate dies so hard, it can happen very easily in any age that predestination becomes perverted into a mere fatalism. It can be so misunderstood as to lead a man to throw up his hands in a sense of helplessness before powers beyond his control. Nothing, however, could be farther from the Biblical idea of predestination. For in the Bible, as we have seen in this great chapter by Paul, predestination means *to be liberated from enslavement by mere fate*. It means that we have God on our side — a very personal God, who desires that our minds and wills and spirits should be set at liberty to attain what he expected for humanity when he created it. Even the deadly chain of circumstances that seems to bind us is broken by this intercepting power of God. Who is to say that "what must be, must be"? On the contrary, if God is for us, who or what ventures to stand against us? Predestination, instead of fixing men within a prescribed circle from which they cannot escape, proves to be almost alarmingly dynamic. This, of course, is what accounts for the extraordinary dynamism that was characteristic of Calvinists in their great periods of faith. They set in motion social and political movements that proved nothing short of revolutionary, far beyond what they themselves expected or imagined. They could and did act with the utmost adventurousness in challenging anything that seemed evil. For they were fighting under God's banners; and even if they should perish, in death they were more than conquerors through him who loved them.

Predestination, as interpreted both in thought and action by the Reformers, thus reflected one of the most powerful results of the Christian gospel. The dynamic of the Christian faith from the beginning worked to free men's minds from the ancient sense of fighting vainly against the stars. Some thinkers have speculated that the growth of modern science is not dependent upon man's reason alone, but was in fact made possible by the sense of liberation that Christianity gave to the ancient world. So long as men supposed that they were in bondage to cosmic forces beyond either their comprehension or control, they could not bestir themselves (as science has done) to subdue the natural world around them. Only a free mind and a free spirit could move forward to change life — life that formerly appeared to be in subjection to sheer inevitability.

History became extremely dynamic after Jesus Christ had been here on earth. Arts and sciences sprang up with amazing rapidity among peoples who at the beginning of the Christian era were barbarous. This dynamism is to be understood only as the act of God, intervening in human history to bring creation out of bondage. Predestination is a way of saying that God was at work, not to restrict men but to liberate them. It is a way of saying that superstition and pessimism and defeatism became inappropriate after God had visited his people to give them, not merely " a second chance," but so far as we know, an indefinite number of chances to make something out of life. In more personal terms, it is a way of saying that God is fighting for me to release me from all that I have been and done in days gone by. Predestination has a way of saying that I am not ruled by nature, or chance, or circumstance, but am subject only to the will of God who has in Christ set my feet upon a new path.

This same intervention, it must not be forgotten, set the

human mind and spirit loose to commit greater ravages than ever upon earth. For what men were predestined to in Christ was *freedom*. Fatalism could be left behind. Ahead were all the risks of liberty — liberty to be human, liberty to take advantage of the new stature of mankind for good or ill, liberty to bring the whole earth under control, and possibly liberty to destroy humanity in doing so. In any case, it is toward this new dynamic that the Biblical doctrine of predestination points. Instead of the spirit of slavery, we are given the spirit of Sonship and made heirs of God. Instead of opposing the fates in vain, we are encouraged to challenge the universe, knowing that God and God alone will decide the outcome. Predestination dares us, as it were, to live both hopefully and dangerously, not as victims of circumstances but as free men.

7

Does It Matter What We Believe at All?

Now that we have gone to the trouble of considering some of the most difficult problems that face Christians who try to think about their faith, it is disturbing to realize that we have not yet faced what is perhaps the most serious "barrier to belief" of all.

This barrier is the feeling that when all is said and done, it does not greatly matter *what* we believe about these or any other questions of doctrine. What if we have indeed said something true about miracles, the divinity of Jesus, or predestination, only to find that it makes no real difference what we think regarding such subjects? What if we have given a reasonably good account of what the Bible teaches concerning the Kingdom of God, or have offered some valid insights pertaining to heaven and hell, only to discover that all this has no practical importance for the human race? What if it turns out that theology, no matter how conscientiously pursued, is irrelevant to what really matters?

It is curious that these misgivings should arise and should have to be faced as a problem. For such qualms seem to arise only in connection with Christian belief, and not with our other beliefs. Obviously, it makes a world of difference whether we believe in democracy or communism. Manifestly it matters whether we believe in monogamy or polygamy. Clearly, it is of great moment whether we hold to moral values or assume that we ought to obey our elemental impulses. Yet when it comes to questions of Christian faith, many people wonder whether it is of any importance to be precise and rigorous in defining, upholding, and clinging to basic articles of belief.

It is strange, surely, that we should hesitate a moment over declaring the supreme importance of Christian belief for human life. Why should there be any question about this importance? More times than one would care to count, it has been argued that since a man's beliefs determine what he does, obviously everybody ought to be as clear and accurate about his beliefs as possible. For, the argument runs, to think rightly about God and man is the condition of saying and doing what is right.

Correct Doctrine and Practical Confusion

It sounds plausible.

But common sense and a look about us indicate that it may not be. For the situation is not quite the same as with certain other kinds of belief. You can probably predict with some accuracy how committed communists are going to act; and you can assume with some assurance that faithful adherents of democracy will find themselves in the opposite camp. But the behavior of the professing Christian is by no means so certain. You cannot tell just how he will react, or what he will do, in a given set of circumstances.

Two persons holding to what at least seems to be the same theology may take quite different courses in the time of trial or the hour of decision. Orthodox belief is no guarantee at all of a consistent life. It is obviously very possible for Christian orthodoxy to be an intellectual point of view that remains in the intellect and never injects itself into the bloodstream and the nervous system of the individual. Apparently similar theological ideas may on occasion lead to absolutely opposite practical conclusions, with an equal degree of earnestness on both sides. There were pious Christians in Germany who went along with nazism. There are pious Christians in the United States who defend segregation on what they claim are Biblical grounds.

These facts are, to say the least, disconcerting to the theologian; and never more so than right now, when theology is coming into some prominence once again. Theologians, naturally, would like to feel that this newly kindled interest in theology is of practical value. But theology is still apt to look like a matter for the professionals and semiprofessionals to pursue — a respectable matter, to be sure, even a significant one, but not a *fighting* issue in a world where there are so many social and political issues that *are* fighting issues. Can we then describe Christian doctrine, the content of belief, as the thing of sovereign importance to us, when in actual fact our principal interests lie elsewhere in this world of conflict, tension, and distress?

How History Makes Us Uneasy

Certain historical factors make the question still more embarrassing. In the time of the Reformation, it is obvious that theology stimulated men to action. It was, indeed, one of the most potent forces making for political ferment. But during the last two hundred years, it is equally obvious that Christian theology has not been the most active agent in bringing about the revolutionary changes that have produced the world as we know it.

The American and the French Revolutions of the eighteenth

century, so fruitful in establishing human liberty, were not very directly inspired by orthodox Christian thought. Despite our habit of equating Christianity and democracy, the revolutionary leaders of that great period were not for the most part devoted exponents of traditional Christian doctrine. It is, to be sure, possible to establish a historical connection between Christianity and the flowering of democracy. Yet precise theological formulations were not in the forefront of the thinking of the real Revolutionists. On the contrary, many sat extremely loose to Christian doctrine, and some disavowed it altogether. They are heroes now, the outcome having been so much to our liking; but that they were *Christian* heroes, in the normal use of language, is not a proposition that many people would care to defend.

Nor did this rather disturbing pattern cease with the revolutions of nearly two hundred years ago. Throughout the nineteenth century, and again, perhaps even more emphatically, in the twentieth century, it has repeatedly happened that those who were aloof from orthodox Christian doctrine were most energetic in working for the welfare of the human race. Within the church itself, as we saw in our discussion of the Kingdom of God, social passion and lack of theological precision have often marched hand in hand. Probably many of us, in personal experience, have not a few times found that our most congenial companions, and those whom we most admired, included some whose theological ideas were at best eccentric, and some perhaps who had no avowed connection with the church at all. They might be Jews, Unitarians, agnostics, or even adherents of totally foreign religions; but at the point of ethical action they more nearly resembled Christian disciples than many who had never doubted or strayed from the faith of their Christian fathers.

This is certainly not the first time that these disconcerting

facts have been noted. Indeed, these facts were so conspicuous
thirty years ago that they led many people to the conclusion
that Christianity was primarily a matter of conduct, of ethics,
and that therefore doctrine was beside the point. Living, not
believing, became the foremost consideration. The assertion
was often heard, "It's not what you believe; it's what you *are,*
that counts."

This was the period in which Jesus came to be regarded as
no more and no less than a moral teacher and an inspiring example of the good life. God was defined in a great variety of
ways. In intellectual circles there was some predilection for
viewing him as the sum of all meaning, or the moral force behind the universe, or just the universe itself in process of developing. This widespread inclination to cut loose from traditional Christian doctrine was closely related to the concern
about high personal and social and political ideals. Such was
the mood of the 1920's, and even of the 1930's; and the same
thought habits are still influential today. This broadly tolerant
view of religion was, and is, ready to embrace persons of all
faiths, or even of no explicit religious faith at all, as though
belief does not basically matter. It amounts to saying: *one can
be Christian without Christ.*

Nothing Bigger than Jesus Christ

But as soon as it is put that way, the weakness in this viewpoint leaps to the eye. "One can be Christian without Christ"
—but even with Christ left out, it is significant that the idea
of being "Christian" or at least "Christlike" remains. The
point of reference is still the life that flowed from Christ, or at
the very least, his teachings. In fact, it is perhaps no injustice
to say that this viewpoint really looked beyond the much admired teachings of Jesus to his love, his sacrifice, his purity, his

self-forgetting, in which all other human lives are somehow enfolded. Even in denying the centrality of Jesus Christ, his centrality was somehow reaffirmed because he was explicitly or implicitly taken as the standard. Even in saying that others who did not confess him, or did not know him, were as good as those who did, it was unwittingly assumed that " Christlikeness " was the thing most to be commended and desired.

Human lives were meaningful in so far as they were, consciously or unconsciously, related to the life and words of Jesus. It was quite impossible to drop him as the center of all thought and action; for to those who had in any way been reared in some kind of Christian faith Christ remained the norm. Buddha or Gandhi or some other figure of an alien faith might be pointed to, as standing up very well by comparison; but the comparison in the last resort was with the One who did not really have any rival, whose integrity could not be questioned, Jesus Christ himself.

Here we are getting close to the secret of the whole matter under discussion. *It matters what we believe in terms of Christian faith, because it is impossible to think in terms that are more ultimate.* Every effort to set up some system of thought that is bigger than Jesus Christ, and somehow takes him in, is doomed to failure. He is, in reality, the boundary of our thinking. When we come to him we must halt, because we can proceed no farther. There is *nothing* more comprehensive than God's own revelation of himself, the witness to which is in Scripture. Our problem is not to see how this revelation fits into our experience of the universe, but to see how the experience of the universe is related to this revelation. It is from this way of looking at the relationship that we take all our bearings.

All Goodness Is Christ's Goodness

What we have in Jesus Christ is the embodiment of all the
excellence of God — of all his justice, mercy, anger, and compassion. And when we see excellence anywhere — any kind
of justice, any kindness, any sense of duty, any sacrifice of
self — what we are seeing is a ray of that light whose fullness
is in God in Christ. We see excellence in many places — compassion, love of liberty, courage, regard for the rights of others,
tenderness to the weak. We shall not despise it anywhere —
in the pagan, in the heretic, in the unbeliever. If it is really
what it looks like, it is authentic; it is a reflection of Christ,
though Christ's name was never confessed. In him is the
fountain of all good life. He is the light that lightens every
man.

This does not mean that we can now dispense with doctrine.
On the contrary, precisely for this reason we shall be diligent
to preserve right doctrine: not because we never saw good living apart from it, but because to guard the truth is to defend
what makes every good thought and deed meaningful and
authentic. It is like the protection of the reservoir from which
a whole city drinks, though few have stopped to think what is
being done to provide for their thirst. It is like maintaining
government for the benefit even of those who are in avowed
opposition to the government. Whatever is good in the spiritual
insights and ethical content of Judaism, of Islam, of Buddhism,
whatever is good in the ethical conduct and attitudes of any
man even though he is an opponent of the church, really de-
rives from Christ who is the source of all that is good. It was
perhaps even inevitable that many should take the treasures
of Christ and make away with them — inevitable, that is to
say, that many should seize upon the inexhaustible moral riches

that are in him and build up their own independent religions of good works. But these are not really rivals: not if there is goodness in them. They are offspring of a father whom they have not known, or against whom they have rebelled; and he will claim them in the end.

Let us beware lest this sound patronizing: the Jew or the Unitarian or the Buddhist may be a better man than I. But to me is given responsibility for pointing out the source of that " betterness," which, if it is truly better, can only spring from the unsearchable riches of the grace of our God.

Theology with a Bite

There is, of course, another and more pressing reason why it would never do for us to be condescending. If there should on occasion appear to be a finer sense of justice, a firmer grasp of freedom, a more sensitive compassion, on the part of the unbeliever, we may take that as a sign that we have not clearly grasped the very doctrines that we profess. It could even be possible that we have driven others into an unchristian position, a point of view or philosophy that is opposed to Christianity, because of our failure to perceive what our own faith teaches, much less act upon it.

Earlier in this chapter we pointed out the dilemma that faces us when we observe that apparently the same theological beliefs lead people on occasion to quite opposing practical conclusions. Now, to be sure, one can never eliminate from human conduct the freedom of personal discretion, and on many a point it may be no great matter that Christians hold varying views. Good theology is not intended to compel conformity, in either thought or action. But it is obviously a more serious thing when on the basis of Scripture and church doctrine one man professes to find reason for believing in the segregation of races, while another sees the gospel as teaching equality. It is obviously no light matter when some professing Christians are led to favor or even to submit to an authoritarian government (and not only in communist lands), while others plead for freedom.

When these divergences, and many like them, arise, it is an indication, not that theology does not matter, but that somebody's theology is defective. It is a signal, not to abandon serious thinking about the Christian faith, but rather to look at it more closely. We have had, in modern times, a striking example of what is here involved. When Hitler came into power, thousands upon thousands of quite orthodox German Christians were content to go along with the Nazi regime. Their pious and orthodox views did not evidently compel them to ask searching questions about what was happening in their country. There was, however, in Germany a relatively small group of very careful theologians, who for years had been examining Scripture and theology with the closest scrutiny. It did not take them long to sense that what was being promoted by the Nazi movement was a terrifying idolatry, the idolatry of the state. Nor did it take them long to discern that the persecution of the Jews was only the prelude to the inevitable persecution of the Christian church. As early as 1934 this group ventured to make publicly what was called the Barmen Confession of Faith: in which they announced, in unambiguous language, that there was one Lord and one Source of moral authority, and that whatever sought to establish some other Lordship was damnable and to be resisted.

That group was the nucleus of what became known as the Confessional Church. Its members — few in number — made perhaps the most impressive stand of any group in Germany against the Hitler government. They suffered, many of them, in concentration camps, and some died under persecution. But dying, they still stood fast. Christian doctrine had taught them that there are some things that are unacceptable, some things that can only be openly opposed, regardless of consequences.

Theology on Trial

As we look back at it all from this date, it seems an obvious enough moral choice to have made. Yet we scarcely need to remind ourselves that it seemed far from obvious to the vast majority of German citizens then. It was, however, obvious from the standpoint of authentic and well-thought-through Christian faith; this faith happened to coincide with common decency and honor and everyday integrity, over against the elaborate propaganda that paralyzed the thought and better feeling of a great nation. In such a time, to think straight theologically amounted to thinking straight in general.

We also are summoned to think straight, both as members of Christ's church and as people living in a time of crisis. To be misled in regard to political and social issues confronting us today will cast grave doubts on whether we have ever quite seen the point of the faith to which we are committed. It will, in fact, be a self-evident judgment on the church if some who uphold no Christian orthodoxy are ahead of us in perceiving what the true issues are. We have labored hard in the church, in recent decades, to give some meaning to what we call " decisions for Christ " — not the once-for-all decision of the conversion experience, but the daily decisions that every responsible individual must make as unto the Lord. It will have meant a vain and empty labor if so-called " decisions for Christ " should acquiesce in the segregation of races, or look blandly on the misery of suffering and backward people struggling for deliverance, or look complacently at the prospect of war among the nations.

How much it matters what we believe comes to the surface in just such questions as these. These are the tests of right thinking, and theology that does not come to grips with these questions and handle them properly thereby stands condemned. Theology that cannot make up its mind what to do or what to think when men are condemned without trial, when guilt by association goes unchallenged, when people are afraid to speak their minds for fear of what others will think of them, is no better off than under the influence of nazism or communism. Doctrine that does not come to the aid of liberty has lost its connections with Jesus Christ, who died to make man free. Doctrine that does not cleanse and purify the air is itself in need of cleansing. All good theology is practical theology, and all authentic doctrine speaks with a terrible directness to human life. On the other hand, all honor and integrity and courage and struggle for freedom speak with a terrible directness to theology. For " if any man will do his will, he shall know of the doctrine."

Barriers to Belief

LAYMAN'S THEOLOGICAL LIBRARY

by Norman F. Langford

There are many formidable barriers to an abiding Christian belief. Mr. Langford in this volume deals with six of these stumbling blocks — the miracles, the divinity of Jesus, the Kingdom of God, predestination, heaven and hell, and the question: Does it matter what we believe at all? He shows very convincingly how to overcome these barriers and make of them bulwarks instead. " The reader can share with the author the exciting task that is laid upon every Christian, the task of being a theologian himself, working through for himself, with the help of Scripture and the wisdom of the church, a clarification and resolution of some of the problems that impede the clearness of his vision, the sureness of his faith, and the depth of his commitment." — Robert McAfee Brown, editor, Layman's Theological Library.

Dr. Langford makes clearly apparent the real problem underlying each of these obstacles to faith, showing that much of the conflict comes either from a failure to perceive the actual difficulty or from a faulty approach to the question. For instance, in attempting to understand the miracles, persons are likely to consider miracles as if they were magic, or go to the opposite extreme and rationalize them unsatisfactorily as natural but remarkable phenomena. Similarly, there is confusion over the nature of the Kingdom of God. Many people today use the phrase to apply to something very different from what the Gospels teach. A further instance of confusion is the conception so many have of the idea of predestination. Dr. Langford explains here that instead of implying the fatalism so many persons associate with this doctrine, predestination actually signifies freedom.